W9-APR-767

THE HUNGER GAMES

THE HUNGER GAMES

MARTIN HOWDEN

JOHN BLAKE

Published by John Blake Publishing Ltd,
3 Bramber Court, 2 Bramber Road,
London W14 9PB, England

www.johnblakepublishing.co.uk

www.facebook.com/Johnblakepub   facebook

twitter.com/johnblakepub   twitter

First published in paperback in 2012

ISBN: 978-1-85782-681-4

All rights reserved. No part of this publication may be reproduced,
stored in a retrieval system, or in any form or by any means,
without the prior permission in writing of the publisher, nor be
otherwise circulated in any form of binding or cover other than
that in which it is published and without a similar condition
including this condition being imposed on the subsequent publisher.

British Library Cataloguing-in-Publication Data:

A catalogue record for this book is available from the British Library.

Design by www.envydesign.co.uk

Printed and bound by CPI Group (UK) Ltd, Croydon, CR0 4YY

3 5 7 9 10 8 6 4 2

© Text copyright Martin Howden 2012

Papers used by John Blake Publishing are natural, recyclable products made
from wood grown in sustainable forests. The manufacturing processes
conform to the environmental regulations of the country of origin.

Every attempt has been made to contact the relevant copyright-holders,
but some were unobtainable. We would be grateful if the
appropriate people could contact us.

A is for...

About *The Hunger Games*

The synopsis for *The Hunger Games* by the film company Lionsgate states: 'In a not-too-distant future, the United States of America has collapsed, weakened by drought, fire, famine, and war, to be replaced by Panem, a country divided into the Capitol and 12 Districts. Each year, two young representatives from each District are selected by lottery to participate in *The Hunger Games*. Part entertainment, part brutal intimidation of the subjugated Districts, the televised games are broadcasted throughout Panem as the 24 participants are forced to eliminate their competitors, literally, with all citizens required to watch. When 16-year-old Katniss's young sister, Prim, is selected as the mining District's female representative, Katniss volunteers to take her place. She and her male counterpart, Peeta, the son of the town baker, who seems to have all the fighting skills of a lump of bread dough, will be pitted against bigger, stronger representatives who have trained for this their whole lives.'

It is based on the hugely successful book series by Suzanne Collins.

Translated into 26 languages, *The Hunger Games* was first published in the US on 14 September 2008, with the audio book released three months later. It has sold over 2.9 million copies in print, and has also sold exceptionally well in eBook format. Collins is only the sixth author to join the Kindle Million Club, which honours authors who have sold over a million paid units in the Amazon Kindle store, and is the first children's or young adult author to do so.

She was originally only expected to write one adventure in the series. But as soon as she came to the conclusion she knew there had to be a sequel. She explained: 'Something happens to one of the main characters and does something that never goes unpunished, and I knew I would have to go back to the tale after that. Initially I plotted all three books but

I find you learn so much about the characters as you go long it's not good to over plot at the start as you hope to find better things as you go along the way.'

Critics loved the book, with *The New York Times* raving: 'The concept of the book isn't particularly original – a nearly identical premise is explored in *Battle Royale*, a wondrously gruesome Japanese novel that has been spun off into a popular Manga series. Nor is there anything spectacular about the writing – the words describe the action and little else. But the considerable strength of the novel comes in Collins's convincingly detailed world-building and her memorably complex and fascinating heroine. In fact, by not calling attention to itself, the text disappears in the way a good font does: nothing stands between Katniss and the reader, between Panem and America. This makes for an exhilarating narrative and a future we can fear and believe in, but it also allows us to see the similarities between Katniss's world and ours. American luxury, after all, depends on someone else's poverty. Most people in Panem live at subsistence levels, working to feed the cavernous hungers of the Capitol's citizens. Collins sometimes fails to exploit the rich allegorical potential here in favour of crisp plotting, but it's hard to fault a novel for being too engrossing.'

The author of the *Percy Jackson & the Olympians* series called it the 'closet thing to a perfect adventure novel' he has ever read, while *Los Angeles Times* raved that it was 'enthralling, imaginative and creepy'.

And *The Times* said: 'If you are looking for something to grip your kids after an orgy of Xbox, *The Hunger Games* by Suzanne Collins is it... Plunge in because this is a rip-roaring, bare-knuckle adventure of the best kind, and destined to be an even bigger hit than Stephenie Meyer's *Twilight*... It would be giving away too much to describe all the twists this absorbing and morally challenging novel throws up, but it is a real humdinger that adults, too, would love. In the renewed debate about why boys aren't reading, *The Hunger Games* would be the perfect antidote – if only schools had the wit to choose it for a class reader.'

The Hunger Games spawned two sequels – *Catching Fire* and *Mockingjay*.

Amandla Stenberg

Amandla Stenberg might just be a young teenager but she has already earmarked herself out as a star for the future thanks to her role in *Colombiana*. She plays Rue in *The Hunger Games*.

The self-confessed 'California girl, born and raised'

was desperate to star in the franchise after becoming a huge fan of the books, saying: 'All the kids in my class were reading them and talking about how good they were, so I thought I should try them too. I tore through them because they're just so good. I fell in love with Rue right away. I love how musical she is, and how quick and smart she is.'

Quick and smart are traits that Stenberg also shares with her character. To prove this, she devised a clever plan on how to impress director Gary Ross at the audition.

She said: 'I heard that they were making a movie, and I already loved Rue. I called my agent repeatedly, saying: "Please, please, please get me an audition." After my many, many phone calls, they got an audition for me. That was my golden opportunity. I prepared and prepared, and I went in and met with the casting director, Debra Zane, who helped me, before I met with Gary.'

Her mother took some of her clothes and rolled them in the backyard to get mud and grass stains over the garments. To cement the look of a poverty stricken youngster, she also put twigs in her hair. Ross was suitably impressed, telling her that he couldn't believe she had her own hair, makeup and wardrobe department!

She added: 'I just discussed how much I connected with the character. I also told them how I've done parkour work, so I have some tree-jumping skills.'

Born on 23 October 1998, Amandla Stenberg was named after the Zulu word for power. She was destined for fame almost immediately, landing Disney catalogue modelling shoots by the time she was four years old. It was perfect vindication for the confident young girl, who had told her shocked mother that she wanted an agent a year earlier.

In 2010, she landed her feature debut in Zoe Saldana's action thriller *Colombiana*. She plays the younger version of the main character Cataleya Restrepo, played by Saldana. She caused such an impact *The New York Times* said: 'Ms Saldana has one other thing to overcome: the presence of a wide-eyed 13-year-old actress named Amandla Stenberg, who plays the protagonist, Cataleya Restrepo, at the time her parents are gunned down, in the first 10 minutes of the movie. Her portrayal of the future deadly-but-sensitive killer is such a perfect combination of trembling emotion, action chops and deadpan humour that Ms Saldana, no matter how sexily professional her work is, spends the rest of the movie failing to live up to it.'

Saldana, who studied Stenberg's mannerisms on set

to ensure that audiences would believe she was the grown up version, raved: 'It was great to watch her. There are so many things we have in common and tapped into about our character. She blew me away. She was so beautiful and so present, but the killer was there, on the prowl. I thought, "I'd better bring my game, because she is bringing it".'

Stenberg is also a keen musician, stating: 'I come from a very musical family. My dad taught me to play guitar. I play violin and drums as well. I started the violin in elementary school. Drums actually came when I was in a programme called *Rock Star*, which was really awesome. We were doing a song by the *Ramones*, so I thought, "Why not play the drums?"'

Despite starring in a huge blockbuster, she's not set on just being an actress. 'I'm not sure. I love all kinds of art,' she explained. 'I mean, I love sketching and acting and music. There are so many doors open to me, I could go in any direction.'

Action Scenes

Heartbreaking loss, romance, and betrayal are all big themes of *The Hunger Games*, the Hollywood blockbuster based on Suzanne Collins's best-selling book series. However, you don't make a story about teenagers having to compete in a violent tournament without throwing a few action scenes in. Buoyed by Collins's prose, *The Hunger Games* has several breath-taking action scenes. Amandla Stenberg, who plays Rue in the film, raved: 'There are lots of crazy things in the movie. Once I got stung by bees – not as a part of the movie, but I just got stung! So that was something I had to overcome, but I don't think that there's anything that traumatic.'

The actors were put through their paces for the movie, with the main cast being taught screen fighting and weapon training to ensure authenticity. According to *E! Online*, the cast were also thrown into stunt boot camp, with a source saying: 'They have to learn archery, sword fighting, martial arts and the like. They want the actors to genuinely know what they are doing.'

Stunt co-ordinator Allan Poppleton told *Teen Ink*: 'It starts with script/treatment, which would outline the fight. I would gather information from different departments, like armoury, costume, art, location, etc. From there, I throw in my intellectual property and then take that along to meet with the director. Then I will start choreographing; then teach the doubles or performers, and then film the rehearsals to then show to the director. Once he has signed off on the fight, I begin to teach the actors. Once they have learned it, I see it through on set with the filming of it.'

Lawrence received praise for her archery skills from iconic rocker Ted Nugent. The keen outdoors man praised: 'All of us archers and bowhunters are happy to see real honest-to-god archery form being displayed properly for a change. Proper archery is one of life's most beautiful ballets, especially when executed by a beautiful woman like Jennifer. It makes for the ultimate eye-candy.'

Anticipation

As soon as it was announced that there was going to be a movie of *The Hunger Games*, media sites were frothing at the mouth in anticipation of its release in March 2012. *Collider* being one, saying: 'If you've read the books, you know that Suzanne Collins's *Hunger Games* universe is ripe for a feature film adaptation. It's epic in scope, has multiple thrilling and unique action set-pieces, and centres on teenagers fighting each other to death with a hotchpotch of weapons/modes of murdering at their disposal. Judging from the full-length trailer, it looks like director Gary Ross has the tone-down pat, but Lionsgate are keeping the second and third act (i.e., the killing, running, and fighting) close to the vest. Hopefully the film takes what made the books so damn addictive – intriguing characters and a twisty plot – and expands upon them, giving us an all-out dystopian adventure.'

MTV said it was the most anticipated movie of 2012, as did several other publications. Lionsgate cleverly stoked up the anticipation from the start, throwing down breadcrumbs at a gradual pace. Before anyone had been cast the release date was announced. Fan sites began thrashing out names for who will play the characters in the book. Despite the clamour for news, Lionsgate chose to cast actors over a period of months, with each actor announced delightfully seized upon by its loyal fans. A teaser trailer was launched, but it did little to satisfy their appetite. A teaser is used just to drum up excitement, but that was hardly needed for this film. Even a series of stills being released over a number of weeks did little to quench their thirst. Eight character posters were eventually released, and weeks later saw the full trailer finally being launched on 14 November 2011 on *Good Morning America*. In fact, there was so much fanfare that the trailer was showed on a jumbotron over New York City's Times Square.

Lionsgate said: 'The partnership, which further distinguishes the film as a major motion picture event, will mark the first time ever that audiences will be exposed to sights and sounds from the film, such as Katniss's home District 12 and the opulent Capitol. With 16 million copies of *The Hunger Games* in circulation, a vast audience of book fans will also undoubtedly tune in for the first chance to hear the beloved characters speak iconic lines of dialogue from its pages.'

Film fans were understandably overjoyed by what they saw, with one exclaiming: 'The trailer does the job tenfold. It was well produced and brought the characters – and the books – to life.'

The cast also couldn't wait to see the final version, with Jackie Emerson, who plays Foxface, saying: 'I think the fans will be really happy. I'm a fan and I'm really happy.'

When asked why she thought it was such a phenomenon, she told *Seventeen* magazine: 'I think it's because Katniss is such a great role model for girls, and also there's something in it for everybody. There's violence, but there's also a big heart to the story. You become so emotionally attached throughout all the books. I think that's really important and the one thing that distinguishes *The Hunger Games*.'

Chief executive of Lionsgate UK, Zygi Kamasa, told *The Independent*: 'The Hunger Games book sales are on

THE HUNGER GAMES A–Z

a par with *Twilight* and we are hoping to emulate that commercial success. The fans are rabid. But *The Hunger Games* crosses over more equally between girls and boys because there are more action scenes, and they're popular with adults too. They make a political statement. The citizens are slaves who are forced to take part in games watched obsessively on television. It's about the dangers of reality television when taken too far.'

It was the most anticipated movie since the first *Twilight* film. But if you think the hype was a lot for this film – what about the next two!!!

Alexander Ludwig

Alexander Ludwig plays Cato in the movie. He calls the character the 'bad boy of the group', and is clearly delighted with that. He told *Seventeen* magazine: 'I loved playing the bad guy. Maybe too much!'

Born in 1992, Ludwig was desperate to become an actor, conceding that he has a big imagination and loves performing. However, his parents were wary of his dreams, worried that child actors become sucked into the shallow world of showbiz. He said: 'My mom and dad were kind of iffy about the whole thing. You know as well as I do the whole kid-actor thing can get a bit warped. But eventually, they said "OK Alexander, if this is what you want, go for it".'

Luckily, he managed to convince them and at nine years of age he managed to land a part in a Harry Potter toy commercial. Through that he found an agent, and several film roles came his way, including *Air Bud World Pup*, *A Little Thing Called Murder* and *The Seeker: The Dark is Rising*.

The latter role saw Ludwig struggle to juggle filming with his education – with him admitting that it was 'really hard'. It was also a tough audition process, he told *Comingsoon.net*: 'I ended up doing about 16 auditions of this part and I've never done that before!

'They sent me the script and told me if I liked it I could go for an audition. So my mum and I went over the script and the second I read it, I swear, I knew that Cato was the part was for me. I absolutely knew it. I'd never wanted a part more. Ever since I've been a little kid I've always wanted superpowers, which are the coolest thing in the world.

'After about eight auditions, I went over my lines and the script on the phone with the Vice President of Fox Casting. It was really nerve wracking – I'd never met him before and we were doing it over the phone, which seemed so crazy.

'After that they flew me down to LA. I'd never stayed there before so that was a pretty cool experience, especially being flown in by a studio. It was really amazing. Once I got there I had to have about three more auditions. I was only supposed to be there for two days but ended up being there for about six and I didn't have enough clothes, so me and my mum had to go shopping.

'Eventually we were just waiting and waiting and it was so nerve wracking, I was just trying to keep my mind off things. Then they called again and wanted to go over the script on the phone in the hotel room, and then suddenly the phone went on speaker, on every phone in the whole room, so they started laughing and that made me laugh too. I felt so embarrassed because it was the Vice President of Fox Casting on the other line, but I couldn't help it!'

In 2009, Ludwig starred as one of the leads in *Race to Witch Mountain*, after immediately impressing the director during his audition. Filmmaker Andy Fickman recalled: 'AnnaSophia Robb was the first and only person I ever had in mind. I loved her work in *Charlie and the Chocolate Factory* but her performance in *Bridge to Terabithia* broke my heart – I thought it was such a difficult role for any actor to pull off. She never auditioned for me… we just had a meeting and rolled the dice. She was born with innate talent, I think, you can't teach what she has.

'Then the bar was raised very high, because I thought: "How do I find a boy to match her?" We had nationwide auditions and narrowed it down to five young actors, but when Alexander came in and auditioned, I just thought he was fantastic. Before the door was shut when we left, we all agreed we should cast him.'

When it was first announced that Ludwig was playing Cato, a lot of fans were concerned that he was too slight for the large menacing character. However, their fears were quashed when they saw the trailer. He noted on Twitter: 'I gained a lot of muscle for Cato because I wanted him to be physically intimidating and I'm not usually as big as I am in *The Hunger Games*.' He clearly loved starring in the movie, calling Jennifer Lawrence 'awesome' and joking that he has a man crush on Josh Hutcherson.

Total Film had Ludwig noted as one of their hottest actors to watch in 2012, alongside Josh Hutcherson and Liam Hemsworth, his co-stars in *The Hunger Games*.

B is for...

The Burning Plain

While 2010's *Winter's Bone* heralded the arrival of Jennifer Lawrence, it was her role two years before then in *The Burning Plain* that showed the promise of the young actress.

Written by celebrated screenwriter Guillermo Arriaga, the film received mixed reviews from critics, and was little seen by audiences – earning only $200,000 in the US. It starred Kim Basinger and Charlize Theron, and *Empire* magazine called it a 'ponderous artistic jigsaw puzzle'. However, those who did see it couldn't fail to see the talent that Lawrence had in abundance.

The film's director Debra Granik recalled: 'This young woman came with a certain stamina and knowledge. It wasn't something she promenaded in the audition, but it became clear to me on set. There was nothing green about her. Her family has been a very supportive nexus from which she operates. Her mum and dad are by no means stage parents and they were probably just as surprised as she was about how fast things can change. Her mother has a really sensible quality though, like it is still going to be important for her to bark at Jennifer and tell her to go and clean her room. Just remember all the normalcy is what makes someone feel sane.'

In the film's production notes, Lawrence said: 'When you first meet my character she's been the *de facto* mother of her siblings for the past four years and hasn't had a chance to be a kid. It's that resentment that really drives the story for the rest of the characters.'

Asked about her acting process in the movie, she said: 'That was one of my first movies, so I had no idea what I was doing. I just memorised my lines and I showed up and was like "Hey, I'm here to shoot a movie!".

'Now, when I do movies, I know what I'm doing. When you get there and you get the wardrobe and you're on set and you start talking to the director, that's when it really starts developing. I don't want to be close-minded enough to already have everything set in stone before I even show up to work. I have my thoughts on what I want to do, but it's also important to be mouldable, to be prepared to try things in a different way, so my character continues to grow through the filming. Before I start filming, I don't have all of the answers, ever. It's just developing, adapting and reacting.'

To retain the resentment on screen about her character's mother, played by Kim Basinger, Lawrence avoided her during the shoot. However, when filming finished they had a big hug.

Battle Royale

Following *The Hunger Game*'s release on the bookshelves, some reviews noted the similarities to the 1999 novel *Battle Royale*. A *Battle Royale* film was released the following year, directed by Kinji Fukasaku, and it told the story of a class trip, which sees the pupils gassed on their bus. Upon awakening they find themselves being briefed on a remote island. They are told that they are part of a Government Project entitled Battle Royale, where they have only three days to kill each other until just one remains. Failure to adhere to the rules will see them killed by their explosive collars. It proved understandable controversy, but it was also a huge hit, prompting a sequel to be made, called *Battle Royale II: Requiem*.

Despite rumours that it was banned in the US, the reason it initially struggled to get a US release was because of distribution worries. There are reports that the makers wanted a wide release of the film, rather than the usual art house style blueprint. However, some distributors worried about the controversy that no doubt would have followed. Distribution Supervisor of American Cinematheque, David Schultz, said: 'If the next school shooting were to occur while *Battle Royale* was still playing, there's a good chance that somebody would get sued.' It was played at US film festivals, however, and has only just begun to get a theatrical release.

In spite of the controversial subject matter, there was still a desire to film a US remake. But the release of *The Hunger Games* has seemingly put an end to that. Film producer Roy Lee, who had been attached to adapt the movie for an American audience, told *Shock Till You Drop*: '*The Hunger Games* took a lot of wind out of the sails of a US version of *Battle Royale* because of its similar storyline, and I'm not exactly sure any studio – even before *The Hunger Games* – would have taken the creative risk.'

Despite the similarities, Suzanne Collins insists she had never heard of the book until she sent the manuscript to her publisher. She told the *New York Times*: 'I had never heard of that book or that author until my book was turned in. At that point, it was mentioned to me, and I asked my editor if I should read it. He said: "No, I don't want that world in your head. Just continue with what you're doing."' She also told the newspaper that she has yet to read the book or see the movie. The same newspaper maintains that 'the parallels are striking enough that Collins's work has been savaged on the blogosphere as a boldfaced rip-off. But there are enough possible sources for the plot line that the two authors might well have hit on the same basic set-up independently.'

Billy Ray

Billy Ray is a veteran screenwriter and director, with his film credits including *Shattered Glass*, *State of Play* and *Breach*. He was attached to write the screenplay for the big screen adaptation of hit TV series *24*, but the script was ultimately rejected because it was felt it wasn't compelling enough.

Unluckily for Ray, his script for *The Hunger Games*

was then rejected by director Gary Ross, in favour of a script co-written by Ross and Suzanne Collins.

Lionsgate announced the news on Twitter, stating: 'The current draft of *The Hunger Games* script was not written by Billy Ray. It is a collaboration between Gary Ross and Suzanne Collins.' When asked if he had any thoughts about the new script Ray replied to *The Wrap* via email that he didn't have any.

However, Ross responded in an interview with *Entertainment Weekly*: 'I told Billy when I began that I would have to put this into my own voice. I wanted to get back as close as I could to the essence of the book and the emotional arc, to get inside Katniss's skin and understand how she grows, largely through her relationship with Peeta. I needed to have fresh clay to do that with. And then, when the draft was done and I got in the room with Suzanne, it was a very, very spontaneous process.'

Suzanne Collins wrote on the film's Facebook page: 'Now that the filming of *The Hunger Games* has begun, I've been getting a lot of questions about the script, so I thought I might share a little of my experience with you. Back in early 2010, Color Force and Lionsgate began the process of adapting the book to the screen and I wrote the first draft of the script. After that, we brought on veteran screenwriter Billy

Ray to further develop the piece. Not only has he written and directed excellent films like *Shattered Glass* and *Breach*, he was a complete pleasure to work with. Amazingly talented, collaborative, and always respectful of the book. His adaptation further explored the world of Panem and its inhabitants.

'As though I wasn't lucky enough, Oscar-nominated filmmaker Gary Ross, known for his wonderful works such as *Seabiscuit* and *Pleasantville*, came on board. As part of his creative process, he wrote a subsequent draft which incorporated his incredible directorial vision of the film. And then he very generously invited me in to work with him on it. We had an immediate and exhilarating creative connection that brought the script to the first day of shooting. Of course, the piece will naturally continue to evolve through the filming, as the actors bring the characters to life, as the entire crew bring their significant talents to the piece, as the editors work with Gary to best realise his vision. The final draft will be on the screen next March [2012].'

In another interview, Collins stated she always knew that she wanted a hand in the screenplay, explaining: 'At the beginning, I attached myself as the first screenwriter. I was writing the third book and there was great secrecy about it and no one could know how it ended. But I knew that if the screenplay got off on the wrong foot, you could end up with something by which you could never reach the events of the third book. And since I couldn't reveal information to the film team, I wanted to be around to keep an eye on that.'

Collins was actually excited about working on a team, because after years spending time alone writing her books it felt like a collaborative experience, much like her TV work. She said: 'It was great, because having spent years in TV rooms, I was used to collaborative writing, and if you're with good people it's really fun. But then with the books, it's been just me talking to me. And that gets a little tedious after a while.'

'There's this certain period of adjustment where you discover if you're compatible,' Collins added. 'But what happened with Gary, it was almost instantaneous. I think we had maybe 15 minutes of discussion, and then we instantly transitioned into writing together seamlessly.'

Bridge to Terabithia

The 2007 fantasy drama movie starred a young Josh Hutcherson and AnnaSophia Robb as couple of 10-

year-old neighbours who spend their free time creating a fantasy world. It was based on the successful novel by Katherine Paterson.

It was a hit with critics, and audiences were captivated by the film's moving ending.

Producer Lauren Levine has stated before that while Josh Hutcherson was not their first choice, his chemistry with AnnaSophia was too good to ignore.

Levine said in the film's production notes: 'Looking for Jess was a real tough hunt. We needed someone who could go from an introverted boy in an isolated world to someone who completely taps into his imagination and becomes a brave leader in Terabithia. That's a heck of a range for such a young actor. And while there are a lot of talented young actors out there, no one else seemed to capture Jess like Josh did. He was able to take the character from the beginning of his journey right through to the end and make you believe in everything he goes through.'

There were several instances in the movie that marked Hutcherson out as one to watch. This was not an overawed young actor, but someone who was confident to try new things to perfect his character. One of his biggest pet peeves as a viewer is when a character is jerked awake suddenly and becomes completely alert within seconds. When he is awakened by his Dad in the movie, he deliberately squinted his eyes to convince audiences he was just awakening.

There was some controversy with the film's marketing, including a trailer that seemed to strongly suggest this was a movie about a fantasy world, rather than in the children's imagination. Producer David Patterson tried to tone down the controversy, saying: 'Although there is a generation that is very familiar with the book, if you're over 40, then you probably haven't read it, and we need to reach them. Everyone who read the book and then saw the trailer said: "What is this? This is nothing like the book. What are you doing Dave?" And I'd say: "You know, what you're seeing is 15 seconds of a 90-minute film. Give me a little leeway and respect. Go see it, and then tell me what you think."'

Despite finding it hard to initially work on a special effects-filled movie ('It's pretty hard when you have to react to a tennis ball on the end of the stick that's supposed to be a giant or an ogre!'), Hutcherson said about the experience: 'The thing I like about this movie is that it's a really cool adventure – but at the same time, it's about how creativity can change your life and about how kids have a lot of feelings and thoughts they need to express. It's about time movies like this were made.'

Cinema Blend wrote: 'Great performances from burgeoning child actors Josh Hutcherson and Keira Knightley lookalike AnnaSophia Robb make *Bridge to Terabithia* a touching and moving film, but the faux fantasy stuff they've shoehorned in around them would have been better left on the cutting room floor.'

C is for...

Career Tributes

Despite the terrible dangers of *The Hunger Games*, some train their whole lives for the chance to compete and actually volunteer to take part. These are called Career Tributes, and more commonly known as Careers. They are also seen as Capitol's lapdogs.

The wealthier Districts, such as 1, 2 and 4, are where you find most of the Careers, where competing in the games is seen as a great honour. It's a philosophy that bemuses the poorer Districts – which liken the act of volunteering to compete in the Games as nothing more than suicide. However, winning the Games in the wealthier Districts brings you great honour and a lifetime of greatness in their District.

Despite their wealth and more training, Katniss finds a chink in their anger: they have been fed well all their lives and when food becomes scarce during the games they can't handle it as well as the ones from the poorer Districts.

Collins's story focuses on the 74th *Hunger Games*, which start off with eight Career Tributes, including Marvel and Glimmer and Cato and Clove. Marvel and Glimmer are from District 1, with Marvel a skilled spearman, while Glimmer likes the bow and arrow. Cato and Clove are from District 2, and are both crazy. Cato is a hulking figure, who can kill you with his bare hands, while Clove likes to use knives. They also play tactical, forming a team with Marvel, Glimmer and a few others to hunt down the rest of the Tributes.

The Careers team up with Peeta to find Katniss. However, Peeta ends up aiding Katniss's escape. Cato quickly becomes the main threat to Katniss from the Careers, and in fact makes it down to the final three. That is until Katniss kills him, as an act of mercy.

Casting

Unsurprisingly, as soon as it became clear that the film of *The Hunger Games* was to be released as a film, it wasn't long before media sites became awash with rumours on who would play the book's iconic characters. One of the big rumours was that John C. Reilly was up to play Haymitch in the movie, a part that eventually went to Woody Harrelson – who in turn was linked to the part of Gamesmaker Seneca Crane. Wes Bentley landed that part.

However, Reilly hit back at the rumours, saying: 'It's a total fabrication. Some jerky tabloid person just put it out there and it was never true. It was not true in any way, shape, or form. One person takes a guess or sees my name on a list somewhere, some assistant sees my name on a list of possibilities for something that I don't even know about, and then people re-post it... People are pretty hungry for any type of entertainment scoop right now, I guess... it's a self-generating kind of thing.'

The toughest task for Gary Ross was casting the part of Katniss. He needed someone who could, in his words: 'incite a revolution'.

Ross said: 'I've talked to Suzanne extensively and I feel like I understand the character really, really well. I feel I know who that girl needs to be. I've read in the press that there are frontrunners, but that's not the case.

'We'll cast the right person for the part. Lionsgate have been great in the respect that they don't feel that they need a movie star in Katniss's role. The greatest thing about the franchise and the books being the star is that we can cast whoever we want. So we all feel like we're just going to cast the right person. What makes Katniss attractive is her strength and her assuredness and her defiance and ultimately her compassion. And I don't mean just physical strength. I mean a real strength as a human being. She knows her own truth. She feels deeply and fiercely. And this is something that the actress has to bring with her.'

Actresses who were being rumoured for the part included *Kick Ass* star Chloe Moretz and Hailee Steinfeld. Moretz said: 'I've read all the books. I'd die to play Katniss. It's such a cool role.'

When Lawrence was announced for the role, Suzanne Collins called her 'powerful, vulnerable and brave'. On 17 March 2011, the press release read:

Lionsgate and the filmmakers of *The Hunger Games* are pleased to announce that Academy Award–nominated actress Jennifer Lawrence will assume the coveted role of Katniss Everdeen in the much-anticipated film adaptation of Suzanne Collins's *The Hunger Games.*

The film will be directed by Gary Ross, and produced by Nina Jacobson's Color Force. Collins's best-selling novel, which has over three million copies in print in the United States alone, is the first in a trilogy of science fiction/action novels that have developed a global following. Lionsgate will release *The Hunger Games* on 23 March 2012.

Newcomer Lawrence's meteoric ascent began in earnest with her breakout role in last year's *Winter's Bone,* and culminated in an Academy Award nomination. This summer, Lawrence will star in Matthew Vaughn's *X Men: First Class* and in *The Beaver*, directed by Jodie Foster. Later this year, she co-stars in the Sundance Grand Jury winner *Like Crazy*.

Author Suzanne Collins weighed in on the selection of Lawrence: 'Jennifer's just an incredible actress. So powerful, vulnerable, beautiful, unforgiving and brave. I never thought we'd find somebody this perfect for the role. And I can't wait for everyone to see her play it.'

'I'm so excited to work with Jen and see her bring this character to life. Katniss requires a young actress with strength, depth, complexity, tenderness and power. There are very few people alive who can bring that to a role. Jen brings it in spades. She's going to be an amazing Katniss,' said director Gary Ross.

The Hunger Games chronicles a dystopic Capitol which requires its 12 subjugated Districts to pay tribute in the form of a teenage boy and girl, forced to participate in the annual *Hunger Games*, a fight-to-the-death live televised event. Katniss Everdeen's little sister is chosen in the lottery to participate, and Katniss volunteers to take her place. Although persevering through hardship is commonplace for Katniss, she must start making choices that weigh survival against humanity and life against love in order to win the games and return home. *The Hunger Games* novel has been on *The New York Times* bestseller list for over 100 consecutive weeks. Foreign rights for the book, published by Scholastic, have been sold in 41 countries.

It might be hard to believe now, but Lawrence's casting raised eyebrows with fans of the series, primarily that the then 20-year-old actress was seen to be too old to play Katniss.

However, Gary Ross was quick to calm fans' fears. 'First, I saw *Winter's Bone*, and I just thought she was phenomenally talented and just kind of riveting and amazing and had so much power," he said. "And then we had a meeting and I found her to be just a completely compelling, intelligent person. Then she came in and read for me and it just knocked me out. I don't want to go into too many details, but we did a scene from the movie and it was so amazingly powerful that it was sort of stunning. You glimpsed every aspect of the role and the potential of the whole movie.

'Suzanne saw every single audition. And not only did she have no issue with Jen's age, she felt you actually need someone of a certain maturity and power to be Katniss. This is a girl who needs to incite a revolution. We can't have an insubstantial person play her, and we can't have someone who's too young to play this. Suzanne was incredibly adamant about this, and she was very concerned that we would cast someone who was too young. In Suzanne's mind, and in mine, Katniss is not a young girl. It's important for her to be a young woman. She's a maternal figure in her family. She's had to take care of Prim, and in many ways her mother, since her father's death. She's had to grow up pretty quickly.'

Suzanne Collins added: 'I watched Jennifer embody every essential quality necessary to play Katniss. I saw a girl who has the potential rage to send an arrow into the Gamemakers and the protectiveness to make Rue her ally. Who has conquered both Peeta and Gale's hearts even though she's done her best to wall herself off emotionally from anything that would lead to romance. Most of all, I believed that this was a girl who could hold out that handful of berries and incite the beaten-down Districts of Panem to rebel. I think that was the essential question for me. Could she believably inspire a rebellion? Did she project the strength, defiance and intellect you would need to follow her into certain war? For me, she did.'

Asked how she landed the part, Lawrence said to *Vanity Fair*: 'I auditioned, which was a long process and involved a lot of improvisation. And then I waited a month or something, where I was convinced I didn't have it – then I got the phone call while I was in London. I was terrified. I knew it was going to be huge, and that was scary. I called my mum, and she said: "This is a script that you love, and you're thinking about not doing it because of the size of it?" And I didn't want to not do something because I was scared, so I said yes. And I'm so happy that I did.'

She added: 'I had read the books before I even knew I would be auditioning for the movie, and was a huge fan of the material. Actually, my mom read them first and thought it was an incredible role and story. She did the same thing with *Winter's Bone*, so she must be a clairvoyant, or just has really great taste.

'Katniss is an incredible character: she's a hunter but not a killer, a 16 year old who's being forced into the arena. These kids are killing one another only because if they don't they'll die. It's needless, pointless, unjustified violence. It's heartbreaking. When I auditioned, I told Gary: "I understand if you don't hire me, but please remember that after Katniss shoots a bow and kills someone, her face cannot be badass." There's nothing cool about her. It's not like she looks around the arena and goes, "Yeah, I got this". I think she looks around helplessly, and thinks, "I made a promise to my sister that I would survive; now I have to kill in order to do so."'

In another interview, Lawrence stated: 'I knew that as soon as I said yes, my life would change. And I walked around for an entire day thinking: "It's not too late, I could still go back and do indies, I haven't said yes yet, it's not too late."' However, she added: 'I love this story. And if I had said no, I would regret it every day.'

The role of Peeta was one of Hollywood's most sought-after parts. Josh Hutcherson was one of the names linked from early on, and he was keen to launch a come-and-get-me plea to the studio. 'I love Peeta,' he said. 'The character is so much who I am – self deprecating, a people person. And he'd be such a great character to play! Like in the third book? Oh my God.' However, while conceding that he had read an early draft of the script and had met with director Gary Ross, Hutcherson said: 'But they're meeting a lot of people right now. One can only dream.'

Other names heavily linked to the part include Alex Pettyfer and Hunter Parrish. Theresa Morgan from *The Hunger Games* fansite *Down With The Capitol* spoke about the choices: 'He's probably going to have to be close to Jennifer's age, obviously. Our biggest concern was that we weren't sure whether a lot of the younger people who'd been mentioned for Peeta could handle the role. With Jennifer being cast, it opens the age range for Peeta.' Hutcherson would eventually land the part and, after coming so close to playing Spider-Man in the new reboot, he would have been understandably delighted at the news.

For the part of Gale, David Henrie, Robbit Amell, Drew Roy and Liam Hemsworth were all mooted. Hemsworth wasn't shy making his feelings known that he would love to star in the movie, telling *MTV News*: 'I read the script. It's a really, really cool story.'

Cinna

The 74th *Hunger Games* is Cinna's first one as a stylist. Everyone assumed that Cinna was assigned to the 12th District for his first venture because it's seen as a lesser District. However, he asked specifically for that District in order to help Katniss. Cinna causes a stir with his designs, leaving the Capitol audience stunned with clothes like Katniss's *Girl on Fire* theme. Her first outfit was a black unitard, with a black cape that had realistic looking flames emblazoned.

Katniss's relationship with Cinna is a loving and moving one – typified in a scene in the book before the 74th *Hunger Games*, where he tells Katniss that if he could bet on anyone it would be her.

On 23 May 2011 Lionsgate announced to the world that: 'Lionsgate and the filmmakers of *The Hunger Games* are pleased to announce that iconic musician and actor Lenny Kravitz (*Precious*) has been cast in the role of Cinna in the much-anticipated film adaptation of Suzanne Collins's worldwide smash hit novel.'

Rocker Lenny Kravitz had met with Gary Ross, but it wasn't until he read the books that he knew he wanted to play the part. He said: 'I thought it was really good storytelling. I'm very much into stories. The character was interesting. I like Gary's previous work. And so I said yes.'

Talking about Cinna, Kravitz said: 'He's very streamlined, very quiet. He knows what he's doing. He's confident. He's got a big heart. I just liked the way he moved – very smooth.'

Kravitz had appeared in TV show shows like *Entourage* and *Sex and the City* and won acclaim for his film debut playing Nurse John in the Oscar-winning movie *Precious*. Gary Ross said: 'When I saw Lenny's work in *Precious*, I was just knocked out. It was quiet and strong and understated and open hearted, all qualities that define this character. I'm really looking forward to this ride.'

For Kravitz it was a way of returning to acting. He reasoned: 'I was an actor when I was a kid, but when I realised music was my thing, I just gave it up. I put blinders on, just focused on music. But I always figured it would come back into my life and now it has I really am enjoying it.'

He added, to the *Wall Street Journal*: 'The thing I love about acting is that it's got nothing to do with me, it's about bringing forth a director's vision. It's like a release. I'm glad it's come back into my life.'

However, like Lawrence, Kravitz's casting raised some eyebrows. He's much older than the character in the books, and fans had thrown about names like *American Idol*'s Adam Lambert and Neil Patrick Harris. Gabby from TheHob.org said: 'While there have been rumours about this casting for a while, we were still a little shocked to learn Lenny Kravitz will be playing Cinna, since he's not who we originally pictured. However, Lenny really brought something special to the screen in *Precious*, so we look forward to seeing him in action in *The Hunger Games*.'

Tanyi from *HungerGames.net* wrote: 'I was taken aback, to say the least. I was thinking someone with a more quiet personality, like Jude Law. On the other hand, Lenny's performance in *Precious* is more than enough to see that he can act with the understated Cinna demeanour.'

However, Arianna Ruiz from *DownWithTheCapitol.net* had no such concerns: 'Lenny Kravitz is going to be an amazing Cinna. He has the flair that Cinna has, yet he also has the calmness Cinna is known for. Gary Ross obviously saw something in Lenny that made him want to cast him. He is not what people expected, but I believe he will surprise people with his performance.'

Kravitz said about playing Cinna, 'When I'm telling kids and they say, "Who are you playing?" and I say,

"Cinna", they go, "Oh you're playing the gay guy." That was an actual answer…That's how they perceived it. So I thought about it, and I read the book and I don't see that he is or isn't gay. He's a designer, he's a stylist, he has gold eyeliner – that doesn't mean anything either way. The question is how far do we go with him? The idea was to pull it back and create a character that's more like a Tom Ford or Yves Saint Laurent – so he wouldn't be too outrageous. He's classic. I kind of played him in the middle. I actually have a friend who is a dancer, who is bisexual, and was a lot more inspiration for my speech pattern and my rhythm, and kind of the way I sauntered in and out a little bit.'

Catching Fire

Released in 2009, *Catching Fire* is the second book in the trilogy.

SPOILER ALERT!

It all begins when Katniss and Peeta are due to embark on their victory tour, following their successful act in the last adventure. She is visited by the villainous President Snow. Needing to quell any thought of a rebellion, he threatens her family's life unless she can prove that her actions were from the heart rather than an act of defiance.

However, it becomes increasingly obvious that their actions have sparked a rebellion, and the Capitol decides to take revenge by concocting a Quarter Quell for the Hunger Games' 75th anniversary. Cunningly, each District must provide a Tribute from among their previous winners, and she is forced to return to the arena.

To stay alive, she channels lightening at the force field, which promptly destroys the area and knocks her out. When she wakes up, she discovers she is being transported to District 13, a place that everyone thought didn't exist any more. She also learns through Gale that, while he managed to get her family out in time, District 12 has been destroyed.

The book saw another rave review from the *New York Times*, with it stating: 'Collins has done that rare thing. She has written a sequel that improves upon the first book. As a reader, I felt excited and even hopeful: could it be that this series and its characters were actually going somewhere?'

Lionsgate have already announced that a film adaptation will be released in 2013. With Gary Ross winning plaudits for his directing duties on *The Hunger Games* it was assumed that he would direct the sequel – with Josh Hutcherson insisting he was the only man for the job. However, Ross went on to quit the project over scheduling difficulties, and was eventually replaced by Francis Lawrence.

Hutcherson said when he heard the news, 'Gary Ross was the best guy in the world. I think he brought so much to the movie. I'm definitely going to miss him. Francis Lawrence is extremely talented. I heard he's the nicest guy in the world. I'm really excited to see what he's going to do with it.'

Capitol

Panem is the nation formerly known as North America in an unidentified future time period. There are 12 Districts that surround the mighty and wealthy Capitol, which is ruled by President Snow.

Any rebellions against the Districts are met with swift punishment, most notably if you are between 12 and 18, as one boy and girl are punished by being selected by lottery and forced to participate in *The Hunger Games* – a vicious television event in which the Tributes must fight to the death until only one remains.

Style and fashion is a huge thing in the dictatorship area, with the vain Capitol citizens undergoing plastic surgery to place whiskers, talons and gold on their bodies in a bid to outdo each other. Other Districts are bemused at the lengths Capitol citizens go to in their appearance. Not only do they flaunt their wealth with their styles and fashion, but with seemingly no thought for the other Districts who scavenge for food, Capitol residents take a special drink that allows them to vomit after eating so they can eat more and more.

When asked what part of the film she was most eager to watch, Jennifer Lawrence told MTV: 'Everything in the Capitol for me. Every time we showed up in a Capitol scene, I was so blown away. It was more than you could have imagined.'

Her co-star Josh Hutcherson added: 'The thing that's cool about the Capitol is that so much of it is practical. Like, the whole apartment scene was all a set they built, which was super incredibly futuristic and amazing. Just to see how that is integrated into the whole green-screen world, as well, is going to be really, really cool.'

Celebrity Fans

Not only are esteemed authors Stephenie Meyer and Stephen King big fans of the books, *The Hunger Games* has also spawned many celebrity actor fans.

15-year-old *Spy Next Door* and *Mr Popper's Penguins*

star Madeline Caroll told *Kidzworld*: 'On my gosh, when I was filming *Popper* I got so into those books. I love those books. I didn't read all the *Twilight* series but I read all of *The Hunger Games* in the course of about a month. I hope the movie does well. I'm very excited.'

When Josh Hutcherson was told that actress Kristen Bell had a *Hunger Games* party for her 30th birthday, where they each dressed up as one of the characters, he said: 'That's crazy. Hilarious. If someone invited me to one of those, I'd have to go as Katniss. That's the only way to go.'

Bell is actually a huge *Hunger Games* fanatic – tweeting: 'Not just 'a' *Hunger Games* fan. THE *Hunger Games* fan. Read both books twice & am silently salivating for the 3rd'. Also: 'Believe it baby! 2nd time I read it aloud 2 friends & did different voices for each character. I am the king of the nerds!'

Even *Twilight* hunk Robert Pattinson is a fan, saying: 'I sort of came across it last year, and I didn't realise it was the most enormous thing in the world. It's good! It will be a good movie.'

Tyra Banks called the books 'sooooo good', while Emily Roberts said: 'I'm really excited to see the movie. I've read all the books, and I've got all my friends hooked. It's totally cool and I can't wait to see it,' Alison Munn posted on her Twitter page: 'Just finished the last *Hunger Games* book… now what do I do?' Adam Lambert hailed the trilogy as 'great', while Emily Blunt said: 'I'm kind of riveted by it and terrified by it at the same time. I can't stop reading it.' *Paramore* rocker Hayley Williams said: 'After carrying it around for two months, I am finally and completely consumed by *The Hunger Games*.'

D is for...

The Dark Days

Around 74 years before Suzanne Collins's story begins, the 13 Districts, tired of Capitol's harsh rule, decided to rebel against the totalitarian government. These times were named as the Dark Days.

The Capitol responded to the rebellion with a swift and deadly reply, including using genetically altered animals named Muttations to attack Districts. During the attack with the rebels, District 13 is destroyed.

SPOILER ALERT!
However, it is later revealed that District 13 made a deal

with the Capitol after stealing their nuclear weapons. They reasoned that rebellion against the Capitol was futile after witnessing their power. However, now that they had technology on par with the Capitol they made a deal to become an independent state and would pretend to be a wasteland to deter other Districts from any further rebellion.

To resume a sense of control, the Capitol established *The Hunger Games*. Forcing young teenagers to slay each other for their entertainment was proof of the Capitol's power.

For 74 years, the Capitol's plan works. That is until the events of the first *Hunger Games* book, with Katniss and Peeta's near double suicide threatening to start another revolution. Their actions were seen as an act of rebellion and the evil President Snow is determined to ensure there is not a second rebellion. He forces Katniss back in the arena for the 75th *Hunger Games* tournament. These events occur in *Catching Fire*, resulting in District 12 being destroyed.

Donald Sutherland

Born in 1935, Donald Sutherland is an iconic actor, best known for his harrowing role in *Don't Look Now* and comedic turn in *M*A*S*H*. The Canadian began performing at 14 as a radio announcer, and studied drama at university, before embarking on an acting career.

The father of movie star Kiefer Sutherland, he has a reputation for being incredibly friendly during making his films, ensuring he knows the first names of all cast and crew members.

It's no surprise that when casting the villainous and cunning man of power that is President Snow Gary Ross turned to Donald Sutherland. This is the man, after all, who played such a brutal leader in a film called *1900* that he couldn't watch his own performance, as his character terrified himself!

Ross ended up writing more scenes for Sutherland after the actor wrote an impassioned email about the character. He said: 'It was a long and thoughtful analysis of the way power is wielded and why. How it controls people and how pernicious the *Hunger Games* were, and the way they were used as an instrument of political control. It was so eloquent and brilliant that it actually inspired me to write two extra scenes for him that I think are pivotal in the movie, and that Suzanne really loves too. I realised that not only were the scenes vital, but they actually fitted a piece that was missing. That was a gift I got from Donald.'

Sutherland and Lawrence only appear together in

one scene in the first *Hunger Games* movie, but Ross promises it will be one to watch. 'It's only when she's crowned that they confront one another, and it's very electric,' he said.

Daniella Churchran

She may not be in the movies, but Daniella became the first actress to play Katniss on the screen. Auditioning for a part for a British movie, the director wanted to audition his two leads. Deciding that the tender scene between Peeta and Katniss in the cave was a great one, that was their audition. But in actual fact it ended up on the internet and was cherished by fans of the books. Churchran would also film a fan video for MainStay Productions, this time the heartbreaking death scene of Rue, who was played by Savanna Kyle Lewis.

Gary Ross was so impressed by the video that she was asked to audition for the actual movie. She had to perform two scenes straight from the book to read, one where Katniss and Gale were talking up in the mountains and the scene between Katniss and Rue where they discuss destroying the Careers' food supply.

While Churchran never landed the part, she also tried to bag a chance of playing Glimmer, telling

DownWithTheCapitol.net: 'I think it would be so much fun to have any part of this film. I think that it would be particularly fun to play Glimmer. She's feisty, tough and I love roles that involve physical challenges.'

Danny Elfman

The regular composer on Tim Burton's films and the superhero likes of *Spider-Man* and *Batman* was signed up to give us the no doubt blood pumping score for *The Hunger Games*. However, just months before the film's release, it was announced that he would be leaving the project for scheduling reasons, as he was too busy providing the score for Burton's *Dark Shadows* and *Men in Black 3*.

Elfman was to collaborate with T-Bone Burnett on the movie, and the Oscar-winning songwriter had said previously: 'He's got an incredible space he's put together. It's the most incredible studio I've ever seen; he's got drums and marimbas and a cimbalom – just crazy instruments everywhere. We're just going to go over there and rock out together.'

Lionsgate Head of Film Music Tracy McKnight said, while announcing Elfman's role in the film. '*The Hunger Games* is such a special property. It has worldwide mass appeal, but it's also sophisticated, cerebral, soulful and rebellious. We needed a composer who can translate these qualities musically, and we have not one but two incredible artists in an absolutely thrilling first-time ever collaboration.'

Instead, *Batman Begins* composer and studio favourite James Newton Howard took over. He said after he finished working on the movie: 'It's a great movie and the director was really cool.'

Talking about his approach to composing, he added: 'I take a project based on a couple things. At this stage in my career, there are a lot of relationships involved. A handful of directors, when they do a movie, it's a no brainer. It's an automatic. You know, it's like a marriage – you're in there for better or worse. And sometimes it's better, and sometimes it's worse, but friendships and creative relationships are established and it becomes very meaningful in that regard. Other times it can be a new director who I'm really dying to work with who perhaps has made a film that I truly admire, and I'll seek them out and tell them if there's ever an opportunity to work with them, I'd love to do it. Sometimes it's just a great script with no money, and I just love the script.

'The first thing I do inevitably is just to start writing music. I generally will write a suite – like an eight or a 10-minute suite just based on my impressions of the script and my conversations with the director. I really started that process when I started working with Night [M. Night Shyamalan], and I've been doing it that way ever since. Night was really the first director I had ever worked with who wanted a lot of music before he started shooting. That really turned out to be a valuable experience. I can't tell you the number of times I've written a suite before they started shooting and then derived significant material out of it and the theme in the final version of the score.'

Dayo Okeniyi

Dayo plays Thresh. He was born and raised in Lagos, Nigeria. He came to the USA to become a graphic designer. 'I have always enjoyed performing, whether it be acting, singing, or dancing,' he said. 'When I initially moved to the United States, I put performing on hold because it felt like it was time to "grow up and be realistic". But the longer I put it on hold, the more the passion grew inside me.'

Okeniyi loved the fighting scenes in the movie. One thing that surprised him was just how much the cast felt like a family to him. He thought it would be more intense given the nature of the movie, but in fact it was completely the opposite. Everyone was trying to out-prank each other, he said, with one cast member coming back to a trailer covered in post-it notes!

Okeniyi was told by the director to think of Thresh as a gentle giant: 'He is definitely the strong, silent type and does more speaking with his actions than his words. However, he does have a gentle side to go along with his rough exterior.'

He said he was excited for everyone to see the film, saying: 'It feels awesome and amazing. I feel privileged to be a part of it. I'm a fan of the books, just like anybody else and I cannot wait for this movie to come out. I've been having sleepless nights because I hope it does well. I hope we've created something that the fans are excited about and that they will get the same feeling that they had when they read the books you know. It's such a beloved book, and I don't want to be part of the crew that messed it up!'

E is for...

The Expendables

Liam Hemsworth is not just aiming to be a heartthrob with *The Hunger Games* movie; he also has his heart set on being an action hero after signing up to the sequel to the surprise smash hit *The Expendables*.

Written, directed by and starring Sylvester Stallone, the film garnered huge attention and excitement during the shooting because of its cast. Harnessing actors from eighties and nineties action cinema, it included Dolph Lundgren, Eric Roberts, Mickey Rourke, Jet Li, Bruce Willis, Arnold Schwarzenegger and current movie star Jason Statham.

The synopsis by the film's company was this:

The only life they've known is war. The only loyalty they have is to each other.

They are The Expendables: leader and mastermind Barney Ross (Stallone), former SAS blade expert Lee Christmas (Statham), hand-to-hand combat specialist Yin Yang (Li), long-barrel weapons specialist Hale Caesar (Crews), demolitions expert Toll Road (Couture), and precision sniper Gunner Jensen (Lundgren). Living life in the fringes of the law, these hardened mercenaries take on what appears to be a routine assignment: a covert, CIA-funded operation to infiltrate the South American country of Vilena and overthrow its ruthless dictator General Garza (David Zayas). But when their job is revealed to be a suicide mission, the men are faced with a deadly choice, one that might redeem their souls...or destroy their brotherhood forever.

Director, co-writer and star Sylvester Stallone brings together a powerhouse cast of action superstars – never before seen together in one film – in Lionsgate's hard-hitting action thriller, *The Expendables*. The film stars Sylvester Stallone,

Jason Statham, and Jet Li, Dolph Lundgren, Eric Roberts, Randy Couture, Steve Austin, David Zayas with Terry Crews and Mickey Rourke. *The Expendables* was directed by Sylvester Stallone from a story by David Callaham and screenplay by David Callaham and Sylvester Stallone, and is produced by Avi Lerner, John Thompson and Kevin King Templeton.

After making nearly $300 million worldwide, a sequel was given the green light. This time Simon West will be on directing duties, with new cast members including Liam Hemsworth, Chuck Norris and Jean-Claude Van Damme. Arnold Schwarzenegger and Bruce Willis will also return in much larger roles.

The plot revolves around Van Damme's mercenary killing one of The Expendables. Seeking revenge, they recruit a young sniper named Billy the Kid, played by Hemsworth. The film is released in August 2012. Hemsworth was meant to be in the first movie too after impressing Stallone, but it didn't happen – however, he was delighted to land his man for the sequel.

Speaking about future roles Hemsworth has said: 'My favourite actors are Matt Damon Leonardo DiCaprio and Will Smith. I love films that they have done. I love *The Departed* and would love to do a film like that. Or a film like *The Bourne Identity*, something that's physical and on the edge. But it's almost impossible to plan out what you want to do. You choose things that interest you, what feels right at the time in your career. I want to do things that I'm genuinely interested in. I want to make good stories and to make the most out of this. You know, I was laying floors for six months, and I can tell you, acting is definitely better than that! It made me really appreciate what I have at the moment. It's been an amazing couple of years.'

Effie Trinket

Showing off her bright pink hair, which is the height of fashion, Effie isn't too happy to be the appointed escort for her District 12 Tributes, as she is used to the luxury life that Capitol offers, and wants to be looking after a more prosperous District. Initially brusque with her charges, her attitude softens.

She is played by Elizabeth Banks. Deciding that she didn't want Effie to be 'too British', Banks decided to make her to be a 'little highfalutin'. She told *Entertainment Weekly*: 'It's a combination of *The Philadelphia Story* and Rosalind Russell in *Auntie Mame*. Rosalind Russell is just amazing, it's one of my favourite performances ever. I wanted Effie to be really theatrical.'

She told *People*: 'She's a very outrageous character. And she was one who was easy to come to because it's all very external – she's all about the hair, the clothes and the make-up. She had very interesting nails, which made it impossible for me to go the bathroom and zip up the dress and type on my Blackberry. I don't know how women who have those nails do it!'

She added: 'I would be in the hair and makeup trailer and I was Elizabeth, and then the wig went on and very suddenly I was Effie. Every day I would have that aha moment, like: "We did it! We found Effie!" Effie is a very complicated woman. She's a spinner. She spins everything into something positive. These kids have been pulled from their loved ones to compete on television in this horrible event in which they will likely lose their lives.

'For sure the biggest challenge of playing Effie was the shoes! All my shoes in the movie are completely amazing but highly uncomfortable. I said to Gary: 'You better be shooting these shoes, because they're killing me,' Banks explained.

Elizabeth Banks

Elizabeth Banks was born in 1974, and she is an accomplished actress, equally impressive in both blockbusters like *Spider-Man* and comedic fare like *Zack and Miri Make a Porno* and *30 Rock* – the latter performance saw her receive an Emmy nomination.

She has claimed in the past that she grew up in a loving but 'lower-middle class' household, recalling: 'We had days where we went to grandma's house for a bath, and it was like "Yay, we're going to grandma's house to take a bath!" But it was because we didn't have hot water, which my parents didn't want to tell us. So instead we had fun nights at grandma's house.'

Banks only ended up acting after she broke her leg playing baseball. Deciding that she wanted something else in her life she tried acting, auditioning for her school play. Roles would stack up, but it was her performance in 2005's *The 40-Year-Old Virgin* that won acclaim, and bigger roles followed, most notably playing Laura Bush in Oliver Stone's George Bush biopic *W*.

She has a short memory, recalling an embarrassing moment: 'Jake Gyllenhaal once approached me in a valet line, and I thought he thought I was someone else. I was confused and frosty and I'm sure I was very off-putting, and he had to remind me that we had met, that we had done a partial reading of *Romeo and Juliet*. I don't have a good memory for names and faces, so my husband now calls it "The Gyllenhaal" – like if we go to a lunch and meet new people, he tells me: "Don't Gyllenhaal these people!"'

Banks has worked with Gary Ross previously, starring in his 2003 effort *Seabiscuit*. Talking about Ross, she said: 'He's a great moviemaker and storyteller. He's a writer too, so every character matters and it's about the fun performances he's trying to get for everyone. I mean, Effie Trinket is an amazing character, so we had a great time figuring her out together. I can't wait for people to see it. It's very different from *Seabiscuit,* but I think all his movies are different. I'm really impressed by Gary's taste in everything; he has such great taste.'

Banks will be seen next in pregnancy comedy *What To Expect When You're Expecting*, which was released in May 2012. She said: 'I cried when I read the script. It has a really great ending: at the end of the movie, everybody has a baby! It really is just a very relatable story for everyone: anybody who is a parent, has considered being a parent, has a baby, whatever. It's just very universal, what happens in the film. We really explore so many great storylines and different paths to getting a child. I had a unique path to getting my son, so I understand how everybody's path to their child is different.'

She added: 'My character, Wendy Cooper, owns a store called The Breast Choice, here in Atlanta, which caters towards breastfeeding. My husband is a dentist, and I imagine that we met during our medical training, and that I studied to be a Registered Nurse, and became a lactation specialist, and then ended up doing that as a consultant, and then opened my own little boutique.

'My character is probably closer than anyone else in the movie to how I feel about pregnancy. I definitely feel that it's an amazing thing that sets us apart from the lesser race, men [she laughs]. But at the same time, I think it's different for everyone and I find that there's a lot of judgment in our culture surrounding pregnancy. I think what's great about my character is that she goes at the judgment head on. She is a very judgmental person at the beginning of the movie and really learns a lesson over the course of it, that everybody has her own experience, and you can't tell people how to live, and you've just got to go through it for yourself.'

F is for...

Fitness training

Liam Hemsworth and Josh Hutcherson may be Hollywood's hottest hunks, and Jennifer Lawrence is a beautiful starlet – but don't think that they could slack off from their fitness regime while shooting *The Hunger Games*.

Hutcherson had to do intense training for the role of Peeta, saying: 'I had to put on weight for the role, which was the biggest thing. I had to build up 15 pounds of muscle and that was done through working out a bunch and eating a lot of chicken and eggs and it was very tiring.'

Hemsworth, meanwhile, had to cut out his normal eating habits, such as going out for calorie-fuelled dates with his girlfriend, Miley Cyrus. 'There is this place in Nashville called Steak and Shake, which is pretty much the best food, ever. That is our secret, sexy place to go. When I look over at her when she's biting into a steak sandwich and there is some steak sauce dripping down her chin, there is nothing sexier than that.'

However, after talking to his brother Chris he knew he'd have to cut back while shooting the film. 'Everyone's pretty hungry, so I wanted to look a little hungry,' Hemsworth said. 'My brother said to me before I started shooting something about me putting on weight. Basically his point was that it was called "Hunger Games", not "Eating Games". That was a wake-up call. I was like: "Are you calling me fat or something?"'

Jennifer Lawrence was no stranger, however, to a gruelling fitness regime after working on *X-Men: First Class*. 'The training was very different. Katniss's is a lot more fun; the *X-Men* training was two gruelling hours every day. I was lifting a lot of weights and I actually lost a lot of mass when I finished *X-Men*, because I was working out so much and was very muscular and strong. But *The Hunger Games* is more fun. It's running and jumping and rock climbing and combat, and all these really cool things. It's longer, like four hours a day, but I don't realise that I'm working... until I pass out! Also, with *The Hunger Games* I need to be smaller and thinner. I do need to be as strong, but my character's younger. Strong arms are something that comes with age, so that had to be taken down a little bit.'

The Future

A bright career is destined for the main cast of *The Hunger Games*.

Josh Hutcherson has two successful franchises under his belt – the *Journey* films and *The Hunger Games*, and he can't wait to make future instalments for both of them. 'I won't be starting again on the next part of *The Hunger Games* trilogy until the summer or autumn, so I have a little time to do something. I'm not a big TV guy, though. I like doing movies. I'd be up for another *Journey*, but I'd have to see what *kind* of journey. It'd be cool to go to the moon. I don't know how it would work technically – lunar gravity would be a challenge – but it would be cool.'

Lawrence will star next in *The Silver Linings Playbook*, a touching, one-of-a-kind comedy about love and second chances adapted from the best-selling novel by Matthew Quick.

The official synopsis is thus: 'Pat Peoples (Bradley Cooper) is a man always trying to look on the bright side of life – the title of the story takes it's name from the expression that 'every cloud has a silver lining'. Released from the hospital after losing his wife to another man, Pat believes this age-old adage is just the ticket to trying to win her back and get his life on track. Trying to remain resolutely undiscouraged, Pat moves back in with his parents and devotes himself entirely to becoming the man his wife always wanted him to be. But it's an uphill battle. Until Pat meets Tiffany (Jennifer Lawrence), a beautiful young woman whose life also has not turned out the way she wanted. Together, the couple will try and navigate through their lives and stay true to who they are, always just one adventure away from a unique friendship, and possibly even love.'

Hemsworth will be seen in *The Expendables* sequel and blockbuster *Arabian Nights* – the latter of which he explained: 'It's about a young commander of an army, who I play. His king gets killed and he has to go off and he ends up teaming with the character Sinbad. My character asks him if he'll come back and defend his kingdom, and they come back. There's some really dark bad guys there and it's an epic film.'

As for Suzanne Collins, she remarked: 'I have a few seeds of ideas floating around in my head but it will probably be a while before one fully emerges and I can begin to develop it.'

Fame

One thing is certain for the stars of *The Hunger Games* – their life changed the minute they signed up for the film. The anticipation for the movie was massive, and that's before the film attracted even more fans.

Lawrence was canny enough to know how much this role would change her life, and thought long and hard before accepting it. 'I think the quick fame is scarier because I don't really work a computer, so I don't ever read comments,' she said. 'That never really scares me, what people think. If I read them, it would scare the hell out of me. What does worry me is how important these things are, and I don't want to offend or disappoint anyone. It's scary, when you think of these huge fan bases behind them and you think you're holding these characters that a lot of people are going to put a lot of weight into. So, like I said, the really scary part is quick fame.'

Asked what might happen if *The Hunger Games* becomes the new *Twilight*, Hutcherson told *Total Film*:

'I'm terrified of what my life could become. As an actor, everyone hopes one day to be that well known, but at the same time to be thrust into it instantaneously is overwhelming. If it does happen, I'll be grateful and terrified at the same time.'

Hemsworth dismissed comparisons to *Twilight*, saying: 'The only was it's similar to *Twilight* is that it does have this huge fan base. But it's a very different story. It's about freedom and family and survival and standing up for what you believe in. It's not presented in a sexy way or anything like that. But yeah, if it does well, it's a bonus.'

G is for...

Gale Hawthorne

Gale Hawthorne is an experienced hunter who has taught Katniss everything that she knows. They work together to gather and hunt the food for their families. They have also pledged to look after each other's families if they are chosen as a Tribute.

Both of their fathers died during an explosion in the same mine, and the first time they met was at the ceremony that followed their deaths. They started out as rival hunters before becoming friends. To ensure his family were fed he often had to hunt for food that was forbidden by the Capitol. This meant he was a frequent potential *Hunger Games* Tribute at the Reaping, a lottery-style competition which selects those who take part in the annual tournament. In the poorer Districts only those that have defied the Capitol are selected.

He is angry about the dictatorship that he lives in, and constantly vents his anger to Katniss during their hunting trips. He is desperate to fight back against the Government but fears for the safety of his family if he was ever exposed by the Capitol regime.

Ross said of Gale: 'As everyone knows, Gale is an enormous part of Katniss's life, but he's not as big a part of the first book as he is the subsequent books. I think he's very, very present and he's tremendously important, but of course we shift into the Capitol and then the arena, where Peeta ends up playing a more prominent role. But he's in her head, he's in her life, he's something that echoes with her throughout the games, as any reader of the book knows, so he plays an obviously prominent role.'

'He's so vital to understanding where Katniss comes from. We need to feel for her and her connection to him.'

Hemsworth saw similarities to his own self, telling *VMan.com*: 'I most recently played a guy called Gale in *The Hunger Games*. He is extremely passionate about standing up for what he believes in, which has always been a strong part of my life. He has moments in the film where he is ready to explode with anger because of the way things are. But because of the consequences of standing up to an evil government, he has to bite his lip and live with it. I've definitely had times in my life where I've had to hold back what I really want to say or do.'

Gladiators

Suzanne Collins is a history buff, and you can see that reflected in *The Hunger Games*. There are many historical references in the book, including Roman times.

She said: 'I decided to base *The Hunger Games* on the nature of Roman Gladiator games. In my mind you need three good elements to make a Gladiator game. You need a ruthless, all-powerful government, you need people forced to fight to the death and you need it to be a popular entertainment and all three of these elements are combined in *The Hunger Games*.'

She added: 'In keeping with the classical roots, I send my Tributes into an updated version of the Roman gladiator games, which entails a ruthless government forcing people to fight to the death as popular entertainment.'

In another interview she stated: 'But once *The Hunger Games* story takes off, I actually would say that the historical figure of Spartacus really becomes more of a model for the arc of the three books, for Katniss. We don't know a lot of details about his life, but Spartacus was a gladiator who broke out of the arena and led a rebellion against an oppressive government that led to what is called the Third Servile War. He caused the Romans quite a bit of trouble – and, ultimately, he died for it.'

Other influences from that period include the term *Breads and Circuses*, which is used to signify appeasing a large population with simple diverting pleasures rather than things that they actually need. The Latin term is *Panem et Circenses*, with the former word the name of the nation where Collins's characters lives. The meaning of the term is similar to the motives of Capitol, which uses entertainment to deflect from their poverty-ridden life.

Gary Ross

Growing up in Hollywood, and with a father that penned the iconic *Creature From the Black Lagoon*, it was no surprise that Gary Ross would have a career in the film world. The Oscar nominated writer wrote classic movies like *Big* and *Dave*, and was one of Hollywood's most popular script doctors. He was also an acclaimed director, making his debut in the excellent *Pleasantville*.

The 1998 movie featured two teenagers being sucked into a black and white idyllic sitcom, based in the 1950s.

Ross said about the movie: 'It took place over such a long period of time. I had kind of the *Alice In Wonderland* idea – you know, two modern kids going through a looking glass. Which, of course, has got to be a TV. What else would it be? I had this satirical way in. Everyone always evokes the 1950s nostalgically as this perfect era. There was no strife; it was a kinder, gentler time, when America was really happy and well-adjusted and mighty and potent. I thought that was a lie, so I wanted to satirise that sort of perfection.

'That was just my first way in, as pure satire: What would happen if we made this perfect era in our memories grotesque? The groaning boredom of breakfast foods on the table, how in Pleasantville it's always 72 degrees, it never rains, the firemen just rescue cats out of trees, no one has any sex, there are no toilets in the bathrooms, that kind of stuff. That's a fun thing to do, but it's sort of one joke. It then led me to ask, what if I injected real life into that? What if I took this perfectly balanced world that has this kind of stasis to it, this world of our memory that never existed, and injected real life into it? Then what would happen? That's when the colour metaphor occurred to me. As soon as that happened, the whole thing started blowing up.'

In March 2010, producer Nina Jacobson announced that several directors were interested in helming the eagerly awaited movie of *The Hunger Games*, reportedly including *The Twilight Saga: Eclipse* director David Slade and Sam Mendes.

Gary Ross had devoured the trilogy thanks to his children and flew over to London to meet producer Jacobson, who was busy working on romantic drama *One Day*. Unfortunately for Ross, he wasn't the first director courting Jacobson's attention. She feared that some directors would ignore the human side. There was great visual scope for the film, and there were plenty of breathtaking action scenes that could be had with the film. However, Jacobson was adamant that this movie would not portray the violence on offer irresponsibly and put visual wow over the character of Katniss. Luckily, she felt that Ross could tackle both sides perfectly.

It helped that Ross had filmed his children explaining why they liked the book so much.

Jacobson said: 'What was amazing was how insightful these kids were about this book and about Katniss as a character. It was so clear that Gary was interested in what the fans cared about.

'In terms of his understanding of Katniss, he has twin teenage children who are a boy and girl. I felt he understood the duality of her character. She's not a traditional heroine, in that frequently heroines are interested in love first and foremost and other things are secondary. That's the least of her concerns. And yet, she is a girl. She's not a boy in a dress. He seemed to understand her impulse toward self-preservation and the preservation of her family.'

On 17 December 2010, *Entertainment Weekly* confirmed that Ross was going to be the director of *The Hunger Games*. He said: 'What makes Katniss attractive is her strength as a human being. She knows her own truth. She feels deeply and fiercely. And this is something that the actress has to bring in with her.'

When he had been announced he was stunned to discover that an eighth-grade reading teacher in Texas had instructed her 134 students to pen letters to the director and advise him on how to succeed with the film, urging him not to 'lose the heart of the story'.

Liam Hemsworth said about his director to *Vanity Fair*: 'Gary Ross is amazing. He always has billion of ideas about what he wants, but also has a very clear perspective; he just makes it work. He really does. He's trying different things and making everything look amazing.'

Donald Sutherland, who plays President Snow, raved: 'I'd fight tooth and nail for him. The script is perfect and the directing was terrific.'

H is for...

Haymitch Abernathy

Before the story of *The Hunger Games*, the hard-living Haymitch Abernathy was the only living victor of the games from District 12 in the 50th year of the event. Every 25 years there is a Quarter Quell edition of *The Hunger Games*, and usually includes a devilish twist.

In the second Quarter Quell, four Tributes instead of the usual two were chosen from each District. Upon being asked what he thought about there being much more competition than usual, Haymitch remarked to the crowd that he didn't care, as they would all be just as stupid as usual.

It ended up being down to Haymitch and one of the female Tributes from District 1. It was a violent fight, leaving them both injured – him with a slashed stomach by an axe and her with a serious eye injury. She was eventually killed by an axe to the head after Haymitch used the arena's force field shield to his advantage. President Snow was unhappy with the tactic, and ended up having Haymitch's brother and girlfriend killed. Following his win and his family tragedy he turned to alcohol.

Haymitch's first appearance in the book is his drunken appearance during the Reaping. His drunken and angry demeanour didn't exactly endear himself to Peeta and Katniss, but he quickly realises that these two have a good chance at competing in the *Hunger Games*. He offers them a deal – he will teach them everything that he knows, but only if they don't interfere with his drinking habits.

Haymitch quickly becomes impressed with Katniss's skill and bravery, and decides to help her further during the Games rather than Peeta, as only one is meant to survive. However, he forges an inventive and daring manipulative plan designed to keep the pair of them alive by convincing the Capitol that their rebellion is borne out of love for each other.

Haymitch is played by Woody Harrelson. Director

Gary Ross said: 'Haymitch is such an unforgettable character: funny cranky outrageous, sarcastic, impatient, biting but ultimately kind. I'm so grateful we have Woody Harrelson to play him. I can't wait for us to get to work.'

Hair

Style is such a big subject in *The Hunger Games*, so it meant hard work for the film's hair stylist.

Linda Flowers told *Seventeen*: 'Elizabeth Banks, who plays Effie, her hair was a challenge because the books describe her hair as having a lot of colours, like orange and aqua. I wanted to make sure it looked really beautiful and couture-style, not like a Halloween party. It has to look right on screen or else we lose people in believing that this is a really sophisticated and advanced culture of people.'

Asked about the men's hairstyles in the movie, she added: 'We put a lot of wigs on guys. I was using anywhere between 400 and 450 wigs and hair extensions on set. For example, Stanley Tucci, who plays Caesar Flickerman, had a blue wig, just like in the book. Almost everybody had something! You would think that the guys would be easy, but they weren't, especially in the Capitol. And Josh Hutcherson's hair had to be coloured blonde, which is a bleaching process and Hemsworth's hair had to go darker.'

Cherry Petenbrink, the film's hair colourist, told TheHob.org that the casting of Josh Hutcherson as Peeta caused upset from fans at first because he was a brunette instead of a blonde, as described in the books. She said: 'As soon as I met Josh at my studio I knew he was perfect for the role of Peeta, really charming and charismatic! One problem, Peeta was described in the books as a sandy blonde while Josh was a dark brunette. I definitely had my work cut out. It was clear based on the vision of Director Gary Ross his hair could *not* be yellow or orange. I decolorised in two separate visits, and didn't want to alert paparazzi either. The goal was to achieve sandy ash blonde but not trash his hair. Everyone was thrilled with the end result. But of course, I did return Josh to his natural colour when *The Hunger Games* wrapped!'

I is for...

Isabelle Fuhrman

Born in 1997 in Washington, but raised in Atlanta, Fuhrman was welcomed by her Russian journalist mother and her politician father.

A casting director from *Cartoon 9 Network* spotted her waiting for her big sister when she was just seven, and immediately cast her for one of the shows, *Cartoon Days*.

In 2007, she made her big screen debut in the dramatic movie *Hounddog*, and immediately followed it up with *Orphan*. The role as the titular orphan was a prized one, and she saw off hundreds of young actresses to land the part after an exhaustive nationwide search.

The plot is as thus: 'The tragic loss of their unborn child has devastated Kate (Vera Farmiga) and John (Peter Sarsgaard), taking a toll on both their marriage and Kate's fragile psyche as she is plagued by nightmares and haunted by demons from her past. Struggling to regain some semblance of normalcy in their lives, the couple decides to adopt another child. At the local orphanage, both John and Kate find themselves strangely drawn to a young girl named Esther (Isabelle Fuhrman) ...but Esther is not what she appears to be and, concerned for the safety of her family, Kate tries to get John and others to see past Esther's sweet facade. But her warnings go unheeded until it may be too late...for everyone.'

Producer Joel Silver said: 'I think a villain like this is interesting to watch. You wouldn't want to see her in the real world, but it's fun to see her in a movie. She's a psychopath in the shape of a little girl who will stop at nothing.'

Producer Susan Downey said: 'The character of Esther starts off one way – you have to believe that she's this sweet, angelic girl, who's had a bit of a difficult past, but is excited to be part of this new family. Then you realise, no, she's pretty evil, and she has intentions. And then you go deeper into why she has those intentions. So we needed an actress who could pull off all those things. Not to mention the fact that we gave her an accent.'

Silver said about the part: 'During the casting process, we all felt very strongly about Isabelle and I have to say, I think we were right. She is fantastic in this role.' Downey attests: 'Isabelle brought all these different layers – there's such a sophistication about her, and yet also a wide-eyed innocence when she wants to play that. At the beginning of the movie, you completely buy that she's this sweet little girl. Then, as Esther evolves during the story, Isabelle was able to pull off all the harder, edgier stuff, as well.'

Fuhrman said about the part: 'I read the script and it was so thrilling, it made me sit on the edge of my seat, thinking: "Oh my gosh, what happens next?" I knew I wanted to play Esther because she would be such a challenge and a lot of fun, so I dressed up in an old-fashioned dress and put ribbons around my neck and wrists, and went to the audition trying to make myself feel what Esther was feeling like. Esther is very complex. She is sweet and happy one moment, and then in a minute she's crazy and upset and angry. She feels that she was never loved by anybody, like she's a good little girl in a world that is just against her. She feels like she is the victim. I tried to bring all her different sides – her shy side, her sweet side, her menacing side and her weird, kind of crazy side – and mesh them into one person and add my own twist to it. If I make people love Esther and hate her at the same time, I've done my job.'

In *The Hunger Games* she plays Career Tribute Clove. When asked by her fans about the role, she declared: 'I can't believe I'm a part of it! I am so excited. She said learning the stunts was her most fun experience on set, 'and getting to meet such an amazing cast and make great friends'.

Next up she stars in *The Healer*, with *The Hollywood Reporter* stating: 'Giorgio Serafini's supernatural thriller *The Healer*, starring Isabelle Fuhrman, Joel Courtney and James Le Gros, is set to begin filming on 14 September [2011] in North Carolina. Furhman, who is one of the stars of the upcoming *The Hunger Games*, and Courtney, who most recently appeared in *Super 8*, will play teenage twins who go on a camping trip with their father only to become lost in a haunted forest. The film is being produced by Giuseppe Pedersoli and Susan Johnson through Pedersoli's Italy-based Smile Prods. Serafini previously collaborated with Pedersoli on the dramatic thriller *Johnny's Gone*, which will premiere at the upcoming Hollywood Film Festival. Johnson and Pedersoli also recently wrapped the family drama *Eye of the Hurricane*, directed by Jesse Wolfe and starring Campbell Scott and Melanie Lynskey.

More impressively she is set to star in another sci-fi film *After Earth*, which stars Will Smith, who plays a man who crash lands on Earth with his real life son Jaden. Earth has become uninhabitable, but his son must try to save them when his dad becomes injured. The eagerly awaited blockbuster will be directed by M. Night Shyamalan, the filmmaker who has helmed box office hits such as *The Sixth Sense* and *Signs*.

J is for...

Jennifer Lawrence

She was born Jennifer Shrader Lawrence on 15 August 1990, in Kentucky. Perhaps because of the influence of having two older brothers, she was a tomboy growing up.

'I didn't have anybody to teach me how to put on makeup or wear a dress,' Lawrence recalled. 'I wanted to be a girl. I just didn't know how.' She was also the youngest in her family by quite a distance – her brothers were five and 10 years older than her respectively.

Lawrence explained: 'I always understood I couldn't

ride in the front seat, choose what we watched on TV or pick which restaurant we went to. Being the youngest and the only girl, I think everyone was so worried about me being a brat that they went into the exact opposite direction of treating me like Cinderella. I'd slap my brother on the arm, and he'd throw me down the stairs!'

Growing up, Lawrence toyed with the idea of acting, even going as far as to appear as Desdemona in a production of *Othello*. Sports were more her thing, though, playing basketball, hockey and softball. She even attempted a stint as a cheerleader, but conceded she was 'the manliest one'. 'I had the lowest voice,' she said.

When she was 14 she found her big break after visiting New York with her mother.

'The first time that my feet hit the sidewalk in Manhattan, I knew that I wanted to live there,' she said 'My mum and I were watching street dancing and some guy asked if he could take my picture. That picture got sent around to all these acting and modelling agencies, and when we went home to Kentucky, I begged my parents every single day to let me try it. The head of a modelling agency told me I had to choose between being a starving actress or a supermodel. I actually thought it was a real question, I didn't realise she was being sarcastic, and I answered "starving actress".'

Auditions quickly sprung up – she impressed executives at Reese's Peanut Butter Cups so much, they said it was one of the best auditions they had ever seen. But when Lawrence's mother told her that they were probably lying, she thought her dreams of being an actress were dashed. Her mother was no fan of show business, probably acutely aware of how hard it is to make it as a child actress.

Help came from an unusual source: her older brothers. They knew how much this meant to her, and fought her corner. Lawrence explained: 'They said: "Mom went to all our baseball and football games and travelled all around the country for us. She would do it for us if it were sports. This in Jen's sport."'

So her mother agreed that she would move to New York with her, providing that she continued to be educated online. Lawrence added: 'I wouldn't have been happy in high school. My mum always said that school changed me. I went from this happy kid to having anxiety problems. I used to get these crazy cramps. Everybody else could understand what was on the chalkboard, but I felt so stupid the entire time I was there. My mum was on my butt all through regular school, but as soon as I started acting, I knew I couldn't do it unless I graduated with a 3.9 [grade A]. That was my incentive – I locked myself in my room and just got through it. It was actually the first time my mum didn't have to be on at me about it. Some people think I missed out, but I had the choice of being in class or moving to New York... well, I got the childhood of my dreams.'

Lawrence starred in TBS sitcom *The Bill Engvall Show* in 2007 – a show she deemed as 'fun'. Running for two years, the sitcom was co-created and starred comedian Bill Engvall, who played a family counsellor struggling to understand his own family, which consisted of Nancy Travis as his wife and his three children, played by Jennifer Lawrence, Graham Patrick Martin and Skyler Gisondo.

Engvall said about the show: 'One of the things I talk about in my act is that, as a parent, all you're basically doing is keeping a lid on things until the kids go to college. I want my show to be a reflection of real life and the real issues that parents and kids face each day.'

Lawrence played the eldest daughter, Lauren Pearson, and she said about the show: 'We all became like family. It funded my indie career, so I could do the movies that I wanted.'

Her career was up and running, despite having her

part cut out of the final cut of the film *Drillbit Taylor*. The film, co-written by *Knocked Up* funnyman Seth Rogen, originally began as an idea by iconic eighties director John Hughes. However, it was the darker roles that intrigued Lawrence, and she had already earmarked the sort of character she wanted to play. She looked at Charlize Theron's part in *Monster*. Theron was a Hollywood bombshell, mostly used to playing glamorous parts. But she turned heads and shot to Oscar glory by playing the lead role in the biopic of the serial killer. This was the sort of film that Lawrence was desperate to star in, conceding that 'she'd love to shave her head' if the part depended on it. She got to work with Theron on *The Burning Plain*, and impressed everyone on set straight away.

She impressed again thanks to a blistering turn in *The Poker House*, a bleak story based on the life of the film's first-time director Lori Petty – who was an actress in films like *Tank Girl* and *A League Of Their Own*. Lawrence plays a teenage girl who must fend for her younger sisters in a house that belongs to her drugged out mother, who operates a gambling den out of their home. 'The character is the exact opposite of me,' she said in the 2008 profile in *Interview* magazine. 'But everyone should stretch themselves.'

The harrowing film also sees Lawrence's character

raped in the film. She said: 'I was young and I hadn't really done anything else, so everything that I read I wanted to do. But now that I'm older and I actually have a point of view, I can see what an amazing brilliant script it is and how it grabs you and it has teeth and it's real and it's ugly, and all the things that aren't usually appealing really appeal to me. When I was young I thought it'd be fun. It was a movie, I auditioned for it. I got it and then I just started acting. Now I can really look back on it and appreciate it.'

When Jennifer Lawrence won the role of Katniss, she had to see off a staggering 30 actresses who had either read with or met the director. Other hopefuls included Emily Browning, Chloe Moretz, Saoirse Ronan, Hailee Steinfeld and Abigail Breslin.

At the start, however, Lawrence wasn't sure she should take the part, taking three days before saying yes. She was a promising actress, carving out a career in critically acclaimed indie fare – much like *Twilight*'s Kristen Stewart. She suddenly became a media sensation – changing her life instantly.

Stewart once ranted to *Elle*: 'What you don't see are the cameras shoved in my face and the bizarre intrusive questions being asked, or the people falling over themselves, screaming and taunting to get a reaction. The photos are so... I feel like I'm looking at someone being raped. A lot of the time I can't handle it. I never expected that this would be my life. It really bothers me when people write nasty s★★t about me, and the perception is that I don't give a f★★k. It could not be further from the truth.'

'What I say is, why would I want anything that's private to become entertainment for other people?... People say that if I just tell them everything I'll be left alone, but God, you think if I tell people they'll leave me alone? They pick up every little scrap, and that's much worse.'

Lawrence agonised over the decision, saying: 'It was the middle of the night in England, and I was in bed when I got the call. And I was so in love with the books and the script, and suddenly it was right in my face – and the size of the decision was terrifying.'

She added: 'I got a taste of fame from the Oscars and I didn't like it. That's a terrible thing to say, because it's such a tremendous honour. But I went from being normal Jennifer to being at these parties where I couldn't just be the girl making dumb jokes in the corner. Everybody's treating me differently and talking to me differently and I know that they're lying and they they're sucking up to me.

'It was a very bizarre time to be presented with a part that could arguably make me the most famous person my age a year from now. I remember sitting in a coffee shop in London, thinking: "If I say yes to this job, next year at this time people will be taking pictures of me with their phones". And I couldn't find a bright side to it. But I didn't want to say no to a script that I loved because I was scared.'

Her mother was so against her becoming an actress in the beginning, but it was she who helped Lawrence make the biggest decision of her life. 'I called my mom and she called me a hypocrite, because when I was doing indie movies and everyone was asking why I didn't do studio movies, I said the size of the movie didn't matter. And she said: "Here's a movie you love and you were thinking of turning it down because of its size." I thought: 'I don't want to miss out because I'm scared. I never want me being scared to stop me from doing something." But I knew in my heart that I wanted it – it was just about working out all the fears.'

Lawrence said about accepting the part: 'When you're a big fan of the books you're always worried about them becoming a movie, because it's usually a disappointment. But I met with Gary Ross, the director, and I loved every word that came out of his mouth. And I knew that he was the only one who could do it. And then finding out that Suzanne Collins was also writing the screenplay – everything was just so comforting. And I was just so excited about all of it.'

Talking about Katniss, Lawrence said: 'The cool thing about Katniss is that every fan has such a personal relationship with her and they understand and know her in a singular way. I'm a massive fan too, so I get it. She's incredibly powerful, brave and tough – and yet she has a tenderness and complexity. It was very humbling to hear that Suzanne and Gary feel I embody those traits.'

Jackie Emerson, who plays Fox Face in the movie, told MTV: 'Jennifer completely and fully is Katniss, and I can say that with complete and utter confidence. She is the most talented actress I've ever seen, that's a big thing, you know. She's also so funny, really nice, charismatic, she's got so many sides to herself that relate directly back to Katniss. She cares so much about her family and she really devotes herself to everything she does, and that's something Katniss does too.'

Lawrence told *Vanity Fair* about her character: 'Katniss is an incredible character: she's a hunter but not a killer, a 16 year old who's being forced into the arena. These kids are killing one another only because if they don't they'll die. It's heartbreaking.'

Gary Ross also raved about his leading lady: 'She has

such command and control of what she's doing, which is a raw, emotional power – it's like looking into a blast furnace at times, and it literally can knock you back in your seat.'

Liam Hemsworth said: 'Jennifer was great. She is fantastic. Really easy to work with, no drama, really down-to-earth, such a funny girl. I've got nothing but good things to say about her. She really was great to work with. And it always makes it easier when you're working with people that you like and you enjoy being around.'

Josh Hutcherson told *Vanity Fair*: 'She and I hit it off. We're both very crazy people – we don't really hold anything back. We were able to have a really good time, and not let anything get in the way of looking stupid or anything like that. We probably looked stupid about 99 per cent of the time, but we had a good time doing it!'

Woody Harrelson told *Empire* magazine: 'Gary cast Jennifer, and I think he had in mind that she's a really strong personality with an unusually keen sense of humour. There's something in her eyes that you can tell she's a survivor, even though she's young. She just has that in her eyes, and that's Katniss.'

Josh Hutcherson

Born on 12 October 1992 in Kentucky to Michelle and Chris, Josh Hutcherson's house was a warm one that was filled with love – not to mention lots of animals as well, including two dogs named Diesel and Nixon.

Showing off was always a big thing with Hutcherson, even at a young age. From the age of four he would put on little shows for his parents, telling everyone that would listen that this little boy from Kentucky was going to be a movie star. And when he was not entertaining his family, he was using his dramatic talents for other dubious means – faking sickness to get out of school.

It wasn't long before his talents got noticed. He explained: 'I got in touch with an agency through a phone book from Cincinnati when I was nine years old, and told them I wanted to be an actor. My parents were like: "Well, I guess we're going to have to do this with him or else he's going to literally just take off and go and do it on his own!" So I went with my parents to meet an acting coach from New York, who said we should go to California for pilot season. And I convinced my parents to go out there. My mum and I got in our car and drove out to Los Angeles, and we stayed in a motel and started to do the movie business out there.

'The acting coach had a connection to some small agencies, so I met with them, and one of them took me on. I started auditioning and was doing four or five auditions a day, running around town, and getting a lot of call-backs, but never really booking anything. And then finally I got a lead in a small TV movie called *Miracle Dogs* for Animal Planet. And, slowly, the credits started building from there.'

Those credits included roles in *House Blend*, hit US medical show *ER* and *Wilder Days*. A brief role in *American Splendour* was followed by a starring role in the CGI hit *The Polar Express*, featuring Tom Hanks. Talking about working with the Oscar winner, Hutcherson said: 'To work with someone so talented and well respected like him really helped me grow as an actor. He was so down to earth and helpful in showing me what I should do. It was a great experience.'

He also worked with Will Ferrell in *Kicking & Screaming* and then performed voice duties for the animate fantasy *Howl's Moving Castle*. He loved the former movie as it was a sports film, and that is something close to his heart: 'My basketball team was the Beverly Hills high school recreational league champions. We were the most unlikely team of like no taller than six foot tall white guys in this league where there's tons of 6 ft 10 ex-NBA players that played for the Nets, the Bulls – legit basketball players. And we won – I don't know how still, but we did!'

His first live-action starring role saw him play a 10-year-old boy discovering girls in *Little Manhattan*. It was a huge role for him, and one he seemed to have enjoyed immensely, saying: 'I think Gabe [his character] is probably a confused kid for several reasons, one being that his parents are divorced, yet they live together and are starting to date again. The other being that he's just finding out about girls and that's *really* confusing. It makes things hard for him, because things he knew or thought he knew are all changing on him.'

By 14 Hutcherson landed another supporting role alongside a comedy great in *RV*, starring Robin Williams. He said about his character: 'I like playing Carl. He's small for his age, so he tried to make up for it by being tough and going the gangster route. He listens to hardcore rap music and wears baggy clothes. Speaking of rap, Robin Williams is an expert rapper. One day the director Barry Sonnenfeld said: "Robin, go on a riff", and he just started rapping. It's so cool how he does it, because he just thinks of words and how they rhyme. It's almost like he's planned it, but he hasn't. It's amazing.'

Two more fantasy films followed – *Zathura* and *Bridge to Terabithia*, before another role in *Firehouse Dog*, of which Hutcherson explained: 'It's about this dog who is a movie star. He can do all these cool, awesome stunts for these movies. One day, he gets lost during a stunt and he comes into my life and starts to cause all these problems, and through the movie we start to build a relationship together.'

While the lead roles continue to come, Hutcherson was keen to broaden his range as an actor and played a supporting role in the drama *Winged Creatures*. Defending his decision, he said: 'I'm always open to not necessarily playing the leading roles because I want to play roles that are the best character roles. And sometimes it's not going to be a leading role. It's going to be a smaller, supporting role. So, really, I'm open to doing something.'

He would star in two blockbusters – *Journey to the Centre of the Earth* and *Cirque du Freak* – both of which are covered in more detail in this book, as is his superb turn in drama *The Kids Are All Right*. That movie, much like Jennifer Lawrence's turn in *Winter's Bone*, cemented his status as one to watch.

And that status was further enhanced after landing the role in *The Hunger Games*. He told *Vanity Fair* that it wasn't all plain sailing, and that in fact he had to wait for an excruciating period before hearing that he landed the part. 'It was a very rigorous auditioning process. I've been a fan of the series for a little while now, and I went in and I met with Gary and Suzanne and a couple of the producers initially, and I did a little audition. It was great, and I really hit it off with them and felt really good about it. And then a couple weeks went by, which were brutal. And then they brought me in to do a screen test with Jennifer, where I read with her… then I had to wait for another couple of weeks or so before I found out that I got the part. And that was brutal, after doing a screen test. I think it was actually about a week and a half, and waiting to hear anything was just, like, ugh. Because I wanted it so badly, and all that time just lying there, waiting to see what happened, was pretty rough.'

When Hemsworth found out he finally got the part he said he was speechless, and couldn't say anything on the other end of the phone. 'This role is so me. I am Peeta,' he explained. 'His humility, his self-deprecating humour, the way that he can just talk to anybody in the room.

Talking about Hutcherson, Ross raved: 'He kind of reminds me of a young Jack Lemmon. There's this incredible versatility to him; he's wise beyond his years and mature beyond his years, and there's just such a natural ease to his acting. He's so comfortable.'

Hutcherson added: 'I don't read a whole lot of books, because I'm usually busy reading scripts, but *The Hunger Games* books were so good that I literally read all three of them over the course of five days or something. I really powered through them. And while I was reading them, my mind was being blown as to how much I felt like I was like Peeta, and how I felt like I could relate. I've never really felt more right for a character in my whole life.'

Lawrence said about him: 'Josh is so charming, and when you read the books about Peeta being able to manipulate anybody… I mean, Josh could get… well, I don't know a metaphor except for off-colour ones!'

Suzanne Collins added: 'People may get thrown, say, by the colour of an actor's hair or something physical, but I can tell you, if Josh had been bright purple and had six-foot wings and gave the audition, he did I'd have been like: "Cast him now!" He was that good.'

When asked about how he thought the film would be received, Hutcherson told *Vanity Fair*: 'At times when you're adapting a book into a movie, you have to take certain creative liberties to bridge the gap between the two forms of media. And with Suzanne involved, I feel like that can really ease people's minds who are worried about it being changed too much, because it's staying true to the story.'

'There are certain things – like, for instance, in *The Hunger Games* books it's completely internal monologue with Katniss. She talks out loud, or you hear her voice in her head basically talking about how she feels and whatnot. In the movie, you can't really do that without narration…You have to find a way to tell these things without using exposition or without using narration. I think we did that really well, and I think that people are going to be really happy with it. What's cool too is that even though it's a big, action studio movie, it had a really sort of indie feel on set, where we had a lot of creative liberty.'

Isabelle Fuhrman, who plays Clove in the movie, said of Hutcherson: 'Amazing! He is the perfect Peeta! He is as charming and funny as his character.'

Talking about the *Hunger Games* fans, he told MTV: 'The fans of *The Hunger Games*, they're die-hard. They're the best fans in the world, so I'm really excited for them to see the movie. But for me, I stay away from a lot of that stuff, just because I don't really look at it all that much. But I hear some things people are saying, and it's pretty cool. It's exciting to hear people are that interested in something you're doing – it's also a little nerve-wracking, – but I'm on board.'

When asked about how his life might change, he added: 'I don't know how you can be prepared for that kind of thing. People are always going to infer and draw their opinions. I'm ready for people's opinions, that's for sure.'

He added: 'I know it's going to be a big change, but I think if you go about it the right way, you can still have your privacy. You've just got to keep on trucking and make sure you're always being true to yourself. Which is so funny, because that's exactly what Peeta would say.'

He is certainly being true to himself, and fame doesn't seem to have fazed him. He only seems to be hitting the headlines for the right reasons. Hutcherson adopted a rescue dog after it was cruelly dumped at an animal shelter, and was honoured at gay campaigners GLAAD's media awards for his long-time advocacy of gay, lesbian, bisexual and transgender groups. He has been a huge supporter of gay rights thanks to his caring mother, and works closely with the Straight but Not Narrow campaign.

Journey to the Centre of the Earth

In 2008, Josh Hutcherson wowed cinema-goers with the 3D blockbuster *Journey to the Centre of the Earth* – a thrilling re-telling of the famous Jules Verne story.

Hutcherson played Sean, the nephew of Brendan Fraser's main character, Trevor. The film sees Trevor teaming up with Sean to find his missing father, and their journey takes them on an amazing adventure involving dinosaurs, dangerous plants and spectacular landscapes.

Hutcherson said: 'Our characters butt heads at first, but each proves useful to the other as the story progresses. They soon realise they need each other more than they ever imagined.'

Fraser said about the plot: 'With Sean's sudden arrival, Trevor is suddenly thrust into a dynamic where he feels the pressure to assume a paternal role, but, even though he is a college professor, he doesn't really understand how to deal with kids. He can deal with college kids because they don't listen to him in the lectures anyway.'

The hunky actor added: 'People call movies a roller-coaster ride. This one actually was one! It's hopping right off the face of the screen and you're right in the thick of it. It did have that moment right there. Audiences have always shrieked and screamed with delight when we've been able to take the moving image to a place they just haven't seen before and have an audience react to it in a way they just weren't expecting.'

Anita Briem, the other star of the movie,

commented: 'It's *always* better to be the only female on set, of course! No, no, it's a very different experience, but in this, with *Journey*, it was wonderful to only have three characters in the movie. We had a great time where there were only three of us on set. We did a lot of action stuff, discovering the magical world of 3D together, so it was a great journey. I think it makes the relationship between the characters all the more intimate and interesting and the audience can get more invested.'

Fraser said he and Hutcherson got on so well, explaining: 'We did lots of running about on treadmills, Josh and I. One of them was bigger than an 8 x 12 foot table. Now, my legs are long and his aren't as long as mine, and they miscalculated our body weight together. The treadmill was motorised and they couldn't get the motor up to speed – all the time it was just going "R-r-r-rwarrr", way too slow!'

The film performed reasonably well at the box office, and with the end of the first film hinting that a sequel will feature the cast uncovering the secret of Atlantis, a franchise seemed ensured. However, the cast and the film's bosses hadn't actually confirmed a sequel, and because of projected costs the Atlantis idea sunk without a trace.

But fans of the first film would get a sequel

eventually. New Nine Cinema bought Richard Outten's original script *Mysterious Travels*, with an idea to tweak the story of an adventure to an uncharted island that is said to have influenced the works of Jules Verne (*Mysterious Island*), Robert Louis Stevenson (*Treasure Island*) and Jonathan Swift (*Gulliver's Travels*) so it formed the base of a sequel to *Journey to the Centre of the Earth*.

In May 2010, it was announced that *Journey 2: The Mysterious Island* was to be made.

Hutcherson was asked to be in the sequel, the only actor from the first one to be in the follow up. He was excited to be back, explaining: 'It was kind of cool. I felt I had earned my stripes a bit, being the only one remaining from the first film. But it was a great experience. When I heard we were making a sequel, I got really excited and couldn't wait to see what kind of crazy stories that they conjured up.'

When asked if he watched the first film to get back into character, he joked: 'Not so much. I was 14 when I shot the first one, so I've grown up a lot myself. So I kind of re-invented the character a little bit. I think there's a possibility that it was actually more fun to make than it is to watch! We shot down in Hawaii, so it was an amazing location. The whole cast and crew, we really bonded and got really close so we had a very good time making it. We got scuba certified at the beginning to do all the water action required. Vanessa (Hudgens, his co-star) was already certified because she's such a gun, but we all had to get certified. They built this giant 100,000 gallon tank on a sound stage in North Carolina and that's where they shot all the swimming sequences. They actually built the Nautilus inside the tanks – it was pretty intense. It was funny because the first time I saw the movie, as the water goes down in the Nautilus and we take our first breath, literally everybody took a big breath like 'now I can breathe as well"!'

He added: 'It was good, it was really fun. Sean was always a very adventurous guy, and he's kind of been stuck in Ohio since the first film. He hasn't been able to get out there and explore like he wants to. He has a lot to go through in this story – he's sort of going crazy and he's also dealing with the relationship with his stepfather. That was a lot more fun to me, there were a lot more layers to him. With a movie like this, I could pull a lot from my own experiences and my own adventurous side and turn that on full blast. But then there were also elements with the stepfather relationship where I didn't have that issue, so I had to really rely on the script to help guide me to the right place.'

Hutcherson has starred with some big actors in

his career, and this film saw him acting alongside Sir Michael Caine and former wrestling superstar Dwayne Johnson. He added: 'Shooting with Dwayne and Michael was amazing. Dwayne is such a big physical guy that at first you could be easily intimidated. But then when you meet him he's super down to earth, super nice, a really genuine person. He's really a gentle giant, a manly gentle giant. And the legendary Michael Caine – he's pushing 80 years old, but he had more energy than all of us. To see somebody like that at that age, who's that accomplished, it just gives you a lot of confidence as a young actor to know that maybe one day you could be like that. Also, just watching him, seeing how he rehearses his lines a tonne – he really knew his words and was able to play with them, almost orchestrate them. That was really cool.'

K is for...

Kellan Lutz

Desperate to see your favourite *Twilight* stars in *The Hunger Games*? Okay, it was never going to happen, but one of *Twilight*'s biggest stars, Kellan Lutz, told *Insider.com* that he loved *The Hunger Games* script and was desperate to star in the movie. However, he was told in no uncertain terms by the 'powers that be' that there couldn't be a 'crossover' between the two franchises.

US Weekly claimed that Lutz wanted the part of Gale, who is now played by Liam Hemsworth.

A source told the magazine: 'Producers told him they didn't want anyone from *Twilight*.'

Lutz was born in North Dakota on 15 March 1985 to a fairly large household – he has six brothers and one sister. However, despite all his many siblings, he still managed to stand out – and was in fact nicknamed Krazy Kellan from his family members.

Lutz didn't know why, but he was obsessed with signing his autograph as a youngster. He remembers 'just having fun doing it for no reason'. 'I'd always want to sign a cheque when I was younger, it's like I was practising,' he added. Good thing too, because the young hunk actor has certainly had to sign a lot of autographs recently.

Moving 'around the Midwest and landing in Arizona', where his mother re-married, Lutz worked incredibly hard at high school in a bid to make sure he could attend a university of some standing. 'I had so many siblings that it was a financial issue, as far as going to a better school, because of all the boys. So, however hard you worked in school and the scholarships you got, that's where you could go. We had limitations, so I worked my butt off to get to any school in California just because my father had been living there since I was six.

'I really wanted to get close to my father because I never really had much of a relationship with him, I'd see him once or twice a year. So my plan worked and

I ended up getting a lot of scholarships for a lot of schools there, and I chose Orange County's Chapman University to attend. The school was great and they gave me the most money. I was going there for chemical engineering – it's kind of crazy, but I love chemistry and engineering.'

Lutz earned some money in LA doing modelling. He had done some modelling work in Arizona, but he found that in LA it was a lot different: 'I'd been modelling since I was 13 or 14, to make extra money. Once I got to LA, the modelling market was a lot bigger, so I was like: "Wow, you can make this much money? That's 10 times as much money as in Arizona!"'

While Lutz would eventually work for Abercrombie & Fitch, and has recently been the face of Calvin Klein, it's not something he'd ever considered as his ultimate career move. But, while he was sure modelling wasn't where he saw his future, neither was chemical engineering.

He had done 'a bit of theatre stuff for my church, growing up, like every year doing the Christmas play and *Oliver Twist*, and fun stuff like that' – but he thought it was just something to pass the time and not take seriously as a career move. However, being surrounded by so many wannabe actors in LA piqued his interest, and he began taking classes.

In a weird way, Lutz was always destined to play a vampire. He told his agent at the start of 2007 that he should be told of any scripts coming up that featured marines, vampires or boxers. When casting for *Twilight* began, Lutz was in Africa filming the *Generation Kill* TV series.

'At the time, my agent was sending me out for Edward, the main character. I read it and it was just too hard to put myself on tape because I was in a third-world country and, if you sent a DVD, there was probably a one in 10 chance that it would get to America. I don't care about being the lead of everything. I just like playing characters that really grab me. So, when I saw the character of Emmett, I thought he would just be such a cool character to play.'

But the project was already cast, meaning it looked like Lutz had missed out on his dream role. Dejected, he decided to take a break from acting after his work on *Generation Kill* ended. He wanted to take a short time off to focus on spending some time with his family and friends.

However, he was to get a second bite at starring in *Twilight*. Lutz told an interviewer: 'The actor who was playing Emmett fell through, for whatever reason. So,

I said: "Get me in there!". The next day, my agent said: "Your audition is tomorrow. If they like you, they're going to fly you to Oregon the next day." So I went to the audition and five of my other friends were there and, in the end, they liked me and this other guy. Then, it came down to them liking me, just a little bit more. I really think Ashley Greene put in a good word and said I was awesome to work with!'

'I had a lot of people rooting for me. So, they flew me out to Oregon that night, and I had to audition for Catherine Hardwicke at 8 o'clock the next morning. It just happened so fast, and I only packed one outfit. Catherine liked me a lot and said I was her perfect Emmett! I was so excited because I was playing a vampire, I loved the script and I loved Emmett.'

Lutz said he didn't really realise what *Twilight* was about. 'I honestly didn't realise it had this huge cult following, and that there were so many books. I was just excited that someone wrote an amazing script that was so sensual. It's beautiful. It's a love story about a vampire and a human girl, and what they can and cannot do. It was just really cool. So, once I found out that there were books, I did myself some reading and I fell in love with the whole series.'

Lutz stars in all five of the *Twilight* movies and is now seen as one of Hollywood's rising stars. Maybe

Lionsgate might change their mind, and feature Kellan in the sequels!

That would certainly be music to Lutz's ears – he recently stated: 'I love the script, love the movie, everything about it. I feel like *Twilight*'s kind of more girly, and on the romance side and lacks the action, and then *Hunger Games* is very much an action packed movie that lacks some of the romance. I got hooked reading all those books. I remember before they ever started making a movie, I was like, "I would love to be a part of this".' When asked if he would like to star in the sequel *Catching Fire*, he answered, 'That'd be really special.'

Katniss Everdeen

Katniss (derived from an edible plant called Katniss) is Suzanne Collins's heroine in *The Hunger Games*, who lives in poverty with her family. When she was 11 her father was killed in a mine explosion, a tragic event which caused his mother to sink into depression and leave the burden of looking after the family on the young Katniss's shoulders. Desperate for food, she began raking though bins in the more prosperous part of town. Starving, she is saved by Peeta, who gives her some bread. Afterwards, she begins heading to the woods to start hunting for food, and it's there she meets Gale.

On the fateful day of the Reaping she steps in to volunteer for a chance to compete in the tournament after her sister is originally selected. A keen hunter and skilled in survival techniques, Katniss overcomes the odds by not just surviving against deadly and better-trained opposition, she defies the rules by winning the tournament with Peeta.

Talking about the character, Gary Ross said: 'She is just such a compelling character, and her struggle and her evolution is so beautiful. You see the character emerge and grow and have so much strength – she's a very important character for kids, because she starts off purely in a fight for survival, and by the end of the story, she learns there's so much more. There are things more important than merely surviving – like, what does it mean to actually live?'

Katniss is played by Jennifer Lawrence, who said: 'I was a huge fan of the books before I even really knew about the movies. I met with Gary Ross, and we had a very long, nice meeting before the audition. And then by the time the audition came around, we were familiar with each other.'

Talking about how much fun she had playing the role, she added: 'There's lots of training, but it's actually really fun. I've done archery, rock climbing, tree climbing and combat and running and vaulting. Also yoga and things like that, to stay cat-like.'

L is for...

Liam Hemsworth

Born on 13 January 1990 in Melbourne, Australia, Liam Hemsworth is the baby of the family. Alongside his father and his English teacher mother, he had two older brothers – Luke and Chris. The latter is now a famous actor, who recently starred in superhero blockbuster *Thor*.

Chris has admitted he was a bit harsh to his younger brother, piling sweaters on him. 'Then we'd stalk him around our backyard with air rifles and shoot him. I feel like the worst brother in the world. But he had a great time, okay?' Hemsworth doesn't remember it

Jennifer Lawrence, who plays Katniss Everdeen, at the Spanish premiere of *The Hunger Games* in Madrid and promoting the film on Spanish television. The books and film are hugely popular all over the world.

Above: Wes Bentley, who plays Seneca Crane in the *Hunger Games* film, with his wife Jacqui at the world premiere in Los Angeles on 12 March 2012.

Below: *Hunger Games* actors Liam Hemsworth, Josh Hutcherson, Jennifer Lawrence, Isabelle Fuhrman and director Gary Ross at a New York screening of the film.

Hunger Games
director Gary Ross.
He was widely
praised for his work
on the first film, but
has decided not to
direct the second
part of the trilogy.

Above: Liam Hemsworth, who plays Gale Hawthorne, has gained legions of fans worldwide thanks to his performance in the film.

Below: Liam, alongside Josh Hutcherson (Peeta) and Alexander Ludwig (Cato), promoting the film in Toronto.

Wes Bentley attending the LA *Hunger Games* premiere.

Stanley Tucci, who
plays Caesar
Flickerman, at a New
York screening of the
Hunger Games film.

Sisters on screen: Jennifer Lawrence (Katniss) and Willow Shields (Primrose) at the film's world premiere on 12 March 2012.

Above: Josh Hutcherson and Jennifer Lawrence at a special signing event to promote the *Hunger Games* film. Suzanne Collins's novels have sold millions all over the world.

Below: *Hunger Games* stars Liam Hemsworth, Jennifer Lawrence, Josh Hutcherson and Isabelle Fuhrman in New York.

that way, explaining 'I'd bend over to feed the guinea pigs and I'd get a pellet in the ass out of nowhere. It *really* hurt!'

However, it wasn't all one-sided. He admitted: 'When I was a little kid I was a devil. 'My brothers called me 666. I was seriously crazy. Once I even tried to stab them with real knives. Thank goodness when I got to about 10 I started to mellow.'

The younger sibling added in another interview: 'I don't know why my grandpa thought it was a good idea to give little kids a proper throwing knife, but he gave it to us…You could throw it into a tree and it would stick to the tree. I threw it at his head. I was about eight and the handle hit him in the head. We had a fist fight one time…and my mum tried to break it up and she got her finger broken. That was kinda like the low point of fighting. My mum and dad went to Europe for three months and me and my oldest brother, Luke, stayed at my grandma's house and Chris had to stay at my uncle's house, because we were too much trouble to be together. We would have a fist fight about who was gonna sit in the front seat of the car.'

Hemsworth is a surfing fanatic, and during his childhood the only thing that mattered in his life was surfing in his beloved sea. He and his friends would surf before and after school, with the evening spent renting eighties comedies.

After seeing his brother act, Hemsworth immediately thought he could do better. It is a competitive streak with his brother that still remains. He said: 'I didn't get an acting job until the last year of school when I picked up a small part in *McLeod's Daughters*. I only missed one week of school, but when I came back I just didn't want to be there anymore. My head wasn't in the same place and I knew I had to get out. So I left school and went laying floors with my brother whilst I auditioned for parts. I decided that acting was what I wanted to do, and I was lucky that it's worked out.'

He landed parts in Australian soaps *Home and Away* and *Neighbours*, following it up with children's programme *The Elephant Princess*.

He also landed a major part in *Triangle* – a psychological thriller that is described as thus: 'Jess is a single mother to Tommy, who is autistic. Encouraged by her friend Greg to take some time for herself, she joins him and his friends for a day of sailing. Soon, they get caught in a freak electrical storm which capsizes their boat, forcing them to seek refuge on a passing ocean liner. Once on board, they realise that the ship is empty. Jess, however, feels that she has been there before.

'As the group of five explores the ship further, strange things begin to happen. Jess comments on having an incredible, constant sense of déjà vu, footsteps are heard in the halls, Jess's keys are found dropped on the floor and blood trails are seen on the floor. A masked figure stalks the group while Jess attempts to piece together the unfolding mystery, as well as survive. One by one, the members of the group are killed until finally there is only Jess, who faces off against the figure.'

Director Christopher Smith said: 'It was supposed to be an American cast but filmed in Australia, because it was largely Australian money. Originally we were looking at American actresses for the lead role but we were going to use an Australian crew, but then the Writers and the Actors Strikes happened. So, actually by sheer luck I was virtually the only person who was making a movie at that point, and that was why we ended up with all the Australian actors.'

Hemsworth taped a script reading and was seen by Sylvester Stallone, and soon he was on his way to LA. He was meant to have starred in the first *Expendables* film, which was written and directed by and starred Stallone. 'My bags were packed,' Hemsworth said. 'I'd celebrated with my friends. Then we got told that the script got rewritten and it wasn't happening. I was devastated. I told everyone "I'm leaving. I look like an idiot."'

Despite losing out on the *Expendables* role Hemsworth still moved to LA, and shared a run-down Hollywood apartment with his brother. 'Going to the States was a huge step,' said Hemsworth. 'I was always working towards one day going to Los Angeles, because it's where the biggest movies are made and where the biggest directors work, but it was an enormous decision.' He quickly fell in love with LA, particularly the beach areas of Newport and Huntington. It might not have been Philip Island where he grew up, but it meant he could be beside the sea doing his beloved surfing.

He auditioned for *Thor*, the superhero blockbuster directed by Kenneth Branagh. And it was an audition that showcased his rivalry with his brother. Both auditioned for the film, and it seemed that the younger Hemsworth was getting closer to the role. He performed a screen test in full costume – 'It's a hard thing to pull off a blond wig. I won't lie' – and was one of the finalists, with his older brother seemingly out of the running.

However, fate was to be unkind. Chris Hemsworth had been working with Joss Whedon on the horror film *Cabin in the Woods*. Whedon had been hired to work on *The Avengers* movie – the superhero team up film which features Thor, Iron Man and Captain America. And, during a conversation with Kenneth Branagh, Joss mentioned to him that he thought Chris would be a great Thor.

Chris Hemsworth explained: 'Joss is fantastic. I worked with him on *Cabin In The Woods*. He wrote and produced it with director Drew Goddard. Right back when I was shooting the film, there was the casting for Thor. The process was coming to an end and Joss asked why I wasn't involved in it. I said I had been earlier, but that I'd been in and out of it. And he said he'd give Ken a call. They didn't know each other, but knew of each other, and Joss said 'for what it's worth, I've been working with Chris and he's a good bloke.' It worked, and the older Hemsworth brother landed the role.

Liam Hemsworth recalled: 'It's all good. The majority of time in this business we're sort of pinching ourselves. We are brothers and we're always competitive, but it's a good thing: it pushes us and we are always happy whenever someone books something.'

Chris Hemsworth added: 'I was like "Listen, I'm the older brother, you shut up and turn it down!" Truthfully, I'd auditioned and it didn't go any further, and then the next I heard he was being flown over from Australia to test with Ken, and I was excited for him, but also secretly angry. But we're very close, and when he was auditioning, I was thinking: "Look I've got a feeling about this". But we gave and continue to give each other feedback.'

If it wasn't bad enough for Liam Hemsworth, his temporary visa was coming to an end. 'There was a moment when I was sitting at our manager's house with Chris. He'd booked *Red Dawn* and *Thor* in the same week, and we were celebrating for him. But then it was like: "Yeah, and I'm probably going to have to go home in a week." But I didn't want to! I love this town.'

However, he was about to get some much-needed fortune. He auditioned for a romantic drama entitled *The Last Song*, starring teen sensation Miley Cyrus. Not only did he land the role, but the girl. 'What happened *happened*, and we've been together for a while now,' he said. 'She makes me really happy. When you start, you want to be professional, but when you're filming those scenes with someone and pretending to love them, you're not human if you don't feel *something*.'

He said about the film, which was written by *The Notebook*'s Nicholas Sparks: 'I'd seen *The Notebook* before and thought it was a really great story, and then

I got this script and thought it was great too. I think Nicholas Sparks has got the power to affect people in some way or another. His stories incorporate so many different emotions and have really good messages about family, love and friendship. I felt the same way about this story, it's about a girl growing up and getting to know her father.'

He said about Miley Cyrus: 'From the first day we met, it was good. When I came in, I didn't know how big a star she really was. I had seen the show a few times, but I had no idea how big Miley Cyrus was. I guess that was good because I didn't get nervous. So, I went in and read with her, and it was really good. She was amazing to work with.'

Miley countered: 'I got a little bit nervous about how big he was, in height! I was like: "I'm going to have to stand on apple boxes or something." It made me a little bit intimidated, even though I'm usually the one that's intimidating someone else.

'Director Julie Anne Robinson said he'd worked a lot in Australia, that we were going to break him out here and that it was going to be awesome. So, I thought: "Great, he's going to be really good. This is my first film, but he's worked before." And I was a little bit nervous with everything. But then, he opened the door for me and I thought: 'That was good! He's got the part!' Julie Anne said we should at least read with him first, and I thought: "He's got it! I don't care!"

'But I didn't want to be the one that made the final decision because, if he did end up being crazy, I didn't want to be the one to ruin the whole thing. But, he ended up being awesome and it was so fun. I was a little bit intimidated, and it's hard for someone to do that to me.'

The surfing mad enthusiast struggled with one thing on set: 'Volleyball was the hardest thing I've ever had to do. Before we started shooting, they asked me if I played volleyball and I'd said: "Yeah, no problem." And I was honestly really scared to shoot the volleyball part because it takes a lot of skills to play that game and I didn't have them, at all. I said to Julie Anne: "I think we're going to need a double," but it's hard to find someone as big as me! We had days where it was just us, and we were playing pretty good against extras who hadn't played before. We looked okay then. But, we had a day where we had 300 extras there, watching us play against professional volleyball players, and they made us look stupid.'

Hemsworth was desperate to star in *The Hunger Games* and he was delighted to land the part of Gale. He told *Vanity Fair*: 'I feel like the books were just written like a movie. You read it and you can just kind of see everything. Right before I went in to read with Gary Ross, I read the first book and I loved it. I didn't realise how good the writing was.'

When Hemsworth got the call from Ross, he was half asleep listening to his voicemail. 'He said: "You did a great read. Do you want to come and do the movie?" And I was like: "Oh s**t. S**t s**t s**t!"'

While reading the book it was always Gale he wanted to play, not Peeta. 'What I thought was really interesting was – and it's one of the hardest things to think about: one of your best friends, or someone in your family, basically going off to war. And that's kind of what happens to Gale in the first book. As much as he's against the government and wants to stand up to them, he really is helpless. He can't do anything about it. … I just thought it was such a gut-wrenching kind of thought.'

Lenny Kravitz

Rocker Lenny Kravitz has been wowing music fans ever since his 1989 debut *Let Love Rule*, and has gone on to sell over 35 million albums and won four Grammys.

Born in 1964 in New York, it was clear that Lenny was going to be a music star. The multi-talented musician was already banging pots and pans in the kitchen when he was a child. He would take up drums, before learning guitars. 'My parents were very supportive of the fact that I loved music early on, and they took me to a lot of shows,' he said. One of those shows was The Jackson 5 performing at Madison Square Garden, which became one of his favourite bands.

As he grew up, his dream of being a musician never faded, but, frustrated with record labels either telling him that his music wasn't white or black enough, he decided to record the album on his own. Recruiting musicians that he knew, he worked on *Let Love Rule*, a heady blend of sixties rock and funk.

Kravitz's new album, the first for four years, *Black and White America*, was conceived after witnessing a documentary about racism in the post-Obama United States, and draws on experiences his mother and father, an interracial couple, had during the 1960s. 'People used to yell obscenities and spit at them – and this was in New York City, not in the South. So it's about me personally and about the situation with race in this country. Maybe we are beginning to move on, but there's still a lot of people who want to hold onto their old ideas.'

The album was recorded in Paris, with Kravitz adding: 'A lot of it seems to be influenced by what I was listening to in junior high and high school. Soul,

R&B, Quincy Jones and bands like *Earth, Wind and Fire* and *The Brothers Johnson* – these were the types of records that taught me so much about producing and arranging music.'

M is for...

Miley Cyrus

Miley Cyrus was born in 1992 in Tennessee to Letitia Jean Cyrus and country music star Billy Ray Cyrus, and has Dolly Parton as her godmother.

The young Miley was desperate to become an actress after she saw a production of *Mamma Mia!* when she was eight years old, telling her dad: 'This is what I want to do daddy, I want to be an actress.' She would begin taking acting classes, and would end up starring in her dad's TV show *Doc*, before getting her big break at age 11. She auditioned for the role of a character in a Disney TV series –

however, she was told that she didn't get the part of that character because they wanted her to audition for the lead role instead!

The show was *Hannah Montana*, and it made her a household name in both the TV and music world. The show is described: 'Miley Stewart is a pre-teen who just moved from Tennessee to Malibu, and now has to adapt to a new lifestyle. She also lives a secret life as a pop star: Hannah Montana, overseen by her manager and father, Robbie Stewart.'

Conquering both the pop and TV charts, Cyrus signed a four-album deal with Disney and the second season of *Hannah Montana* premiered on 23 April 2007. Her concert tickets sold out in minutes, with a spokesperson for Ticketmaster saying wryly: 'Hell hath no fury like the parent of a child throwing a tantrum. People who have been in this business for a long time are watching what's happening, and they say there hasn't been a demand of this level or intensity since *The Beatles* or Elvis.'

Like any TV star it wouldn't be long before she would try to conquer the big screen as well. First came *Hannah Montana & Miley Cyrus: Best of Both Worlds Concert* – a 3D film concert of the best-selling tour. It was a box office smash, as was *Hannah Montana: The Movie*.

The film's producer Al Gough said: 'Miley is one of those rare, incredible talents. She can sing, she can dance, she can act–and she's funny. To be natural on film is the hardest thing in the world, and she does it without any effort, her instincts are so good. To watch her grow as an actor over the course of making this film has been amazing.'

Her dad said about her success: 'We both just love what we do. She loves acting, she loves singing, she loves writing songs. For the most part with Miley, I think part of it is staying real and remembering who she is and where she comes from and what she's all about. As my dad told me when I was a little boy, it's important to always be aware of your current surroundings and where you're at, at any crossroads of life, and always looking forward to the future and knowing where you want to go. But, most importantly, to never forget where you come from.'

Desperate to showcase a more grown-up image Cyrus would then star in *The Last Song* alongside Liam Hemsworth. She told *Teen Vogue*: 'In LA, I had so many security blankets, people helping me with everything. I tried to book my friend a flight, and I didn't know how because I was used to someone doing it for me. I didn't want a babysitter anymore. I went to film in Tybee Island crying harder than I had ever cried in my life – and I left with the biggest smile on my face.'

Talking about the transition from child star to grown up actress, she remarked: 'When we were planning when the transition would take place, and when I would leave the show behind and do something else, everyone was like: "Well, this is what we think you should do." And I thought: "I've gone these last five years with *Hannah Montana* with everyone telling me what to do. Now, it's up to me and what I think is right in my career, so I'm just going in my own direction." I have to be careful, in a sense, to not lose who I am, or the Miley Cyrus factor, by going to do other characters. I still want them to know who I am, but I want to extend my audience. I want to continue to do what I love, but also give myself new challenges and not just be the same person, over and over.'

She was delighted to meet Hemsworth, saying: 'Yeah. I think we're both deeper than normal people. He's very grateful for what he has, but he doesn't let it go to his head. I'm like that too. He's also a really freaking good actor. And he's cute!'

However, Miley Cyrus's good fortune came at a cost for teenager Laura Griffin. She had been Hemsworth's girlfriend of five years, but would learn that she had lost him to the *Hannah Montana* star. She told *Woman's Day*, 'He was my boyfriend and my best friend. There is no other reason why we would have broken up.' She took to Facebook following the news, saying that she was 'depressed' and had 'tears streaming'.

She had met him at school. 'He was the new boy at school and all the girls liked him,' she said. 'He was popular, a bit of a joker and made me laugh. We became inseparable. He tried to teach me to surf, we watched movies, and went shopping. Liam became more than a boyfriend, he was my best friend.'

Murder Sports

The Hunger Games tells the story of a group of children having to fight to the death in front of a baying crowd, who are thirsty for blood and eager for the next kill as they watch it unfold.

Boys and girls aged between 12 and 18 battle with each other in a mass arena, forced to use their wits, wilderness training and fighting skills in a bid to win the ultimate prize – to live. The participants consist of volunteers who have been training all their life and those who have rebelled against the government and are being punished for their actions.

The Hunger Games is not the only story to feature a

winner-takes-all prize. In 1975, two killer sport films were released – *Death Race 2000* and *Rollerball*.

Talking about *Death Race 2000*, director Roger Corman said: 'The original won a poll as the greatest B-movie ever made. I think it won that poll because of the complexity of the story – it had a little bit of political commentary and humour, but was combined with action.' The film tells the story of society in 2000, being led by the Bipartisan Party following a military coup. To entertain the masses a three-day event is set up each year – a road race, with drivers getting extra points for hitting and killing pedestrians. David Carradine plays the hero, while a then not very famous Sylvester Stallone was the bad guy.

The film was remade in 2008, with Jason Statham as the lead character. Corman said about the remake: 'It had very little. They asked me to contribute my notes to the script, which is about the only thing I did. I read the first draft and I knew they were going in a direction substantially different from the original. So I had my story editor from then on read the script and give notes, because I knew they weren't going to pay any attention to the notes anyway. It was just a way to justify the fact that they had given me an executive producer credit.

'I thought it was a very good action film as it stood.

However, the whole point of the first *Death Race* was the fact that it was a race from New York to the new Los Angeles in the year 2000. We made it in the 1970s, and the drivers were scored on two points: how fast they drove, and how many pedestrians they could kill. And it was very important to me that the concept of killing pedestrians as a sport be in there, because I was thinking of stock-car racing today. They're really looking for the crashes and the flames and explosions as much as they are for the races, and I was simply carrying that over to include the spectators into the sport.

'But they dropped that element from the *Death Race* remake. And it may be that they were right for the kind of picture they were doing, but when I realised they were going in that direction, I felt that there weren't going to be any notes I could give to bring back the kind of social commentary the previous film had. This was a straight action picture, and I left it to them. And as a straight action picture, they were successful. I thought it was a good job.'

The other 1975 film was *Rollerball*. It is set in 2018, in a brutal world that features a hugely popular but violent sport that sees teams trying to outscore each other while skating around an oval track.

The sport's biggest player is Jonathan E, played by

James Caan, His huge popularity begins to make the sport's bosses fearful and, in a bid to prove that no player is bigger than the game, they continually relax the rules until at the final game any violence, including death, is allowed to stop your opponent.

James Caan said about *Rollerball*: 'We broke a lot of bones. We were skating 40 to 45 miles an hour. I wound up doing almost all my stuff. It was great fun! The walking and talking were a little overdone. The burning of the trees – that was bullshit.'

He added: 'I've been lucky, really lucky with the critics in my life, they've been exceptionally nice to me. But there was one critique of *Rollerball*, in *Women's Wear Daily*, oddly enough, which said: "We saw James Caan the athlete, but where was the actor?" The whole point of the picture was that these guys were state-raised, with no emotion. It wasn't a picture for crying and screaming.'

Like *Death Race 2000*, *Rollerball* was remade in 2002. Unfortunately the film, which starred Chris Klein, was a critical and commercial disaster.

The remake's plot is described as thus: 'It is the year 2005. The new sport of Rollerball is hugely popular in Central Asia, Russia, China, Mongolia and Turkey. Marcus Ridley asks NHL hopeful Jonathan Cross to join him playing for the Zhambel Horsemen in

Kazakhstan. The highly paid Marcus and Jonathan are teamed with low-paid locals, who are often severely injured in the game, which is an extraordinarily violent extension of roller derby involving motorcycles, a metal ball, and many trappings of the World Wrestling Entertainment (WWE).

'Soon the team's star and the darling of promoter Alexi Petrovich, Jonathan is thrilled by the high-octane sport, the hype, the sports cars, and his female teammate Aurora. But gradually Jonathan discovers that the cynical Alexi and the opportunistic Sanjay will go to any lengths to manipulate the game in order to provide an ever more gory spectacle and improve the game's popularity.'

The BBC wrote: 'Crass and utterly incomprehensible, this new *Rollerball* does away with the original's political backdrop, turns the volume up to 11, and makes like it was written and directed by a middle-aged version of *Beavis and Butt-Head*. Did the film-makers really believe including a few seconds' worth of *Slipknot* would be enough to fool anyone into thinking that this was a cool movie?

'Just to show how bad things have got in the years since Norman Jewison's controversial original, instead of a macho hard man like James Caan we now get Chris Klein – an actor who usually plays sweet-natured airheads in comedies such as *American Pie* – as the film's hero. Klein's Jonathan Cross is a skateboarder who joins the Rollerball circuit in Central Asia and gradually finds himself at odds with the league's money-hungry owner (Reno). Or something like that. Frankly, you'll realise a few minutes into this farrago that trying to follow the "plot" is futile.'

'I was really disappointed,' said Klein. 'It was my first time working on a really big action piece and we all went out there and tried our best. We had John McTiernan directing the movie, and at the end of the day it wasn't received well. I don't know... I guess you have to sometimes take the good with the bad. Sometimes what you put out there isn't going to stick.'

Feeling that too many people compared it to the original, Klein said it was 'really tough because even though we have the same title it's definitely a different kind of movie. But the way it was edited and finished, and the scenes that we were trying to bring across to the audience, didn't quite work I guess.' Klein denied it hurt his career, but ruefully admitted 'it certainly didn't help it either'.

There was also 1987's *The Running Man*. Starring Arnold Schwarzenegger and based on a Stephen King novel, the high-concept plot is of a cheesy style game show with a deadly twist – convicted criminals are forced to fend for their lives from colourful bad guys.

Yahoo.com wrote: '*The Running Man* is a perfect example of an action film where Arnold actually had to have some talent showing emotion. It's action-packed from start to finish and is one of his famous one-liner films. The film is based, very loosely, on the novel written by Stephen King under the pseudonym Richard Bachman.

'I find it relatively frightening that we are now dealing with several things that were in this totalitarian society. Cameras everywhere, televised entertainment involving pain, CGI technology that could frame someone quite easily, restricted travel, and even blurring lines between government and media. The most chilling revelation is quite possibly that TV isn't your end-all-be-all source of information like the vast majority of Americans think. The media will lie to you, or give you a skewed perspective at every possible turn. The story is amazing, and considering how long ago it was written, is very insightful. This may not be one of the best sci-fi films ever made, but it does deserve some credit.'

Mockingjay

Named after a genetically engineered bird that Katniss has taken as her symbol, Collins's third book in the trilogy sees all out rebellion against the Capitol.

The plot is described: 'Against all odds, Katniss Everdeen has survived *The Hunger Games* twice. But now that she's made it out of the bloody arena alive, she's still not safe. The Capitol is angry. The Capitol wants revenge. Who do they think should pay for the unrest? Katniss. And what's worse, President Snow has made it clear that no one else is safe either. Not Katniss's family, not her friends, not the people of District 12. Powerful and haunting, this thrilling final instalment of Suzanne Collins's groundbreaking *The Hunger Games* trilogy promises to be one of the most talked about books of the year.'

The film of *Mockingjay* is being split into two parts. Lawrence seemed to agree with the decision, reasoning: 'It's always hard every time you convert a novel into a movie because you have to cut so much out. So in a weird way, it's kind of a relief because you get to keep everything in there. But it is more work. We'll probably do them back to back.'

The book was critically acclaimed, with the *New York Times* saying: 'Though *The Hunger Games* trilogy has by now won many adult readers – there are 5.6

million copies of the series in print in the United States and Canada alone – it is the perfect teenage story with its exquisitely refined rage against the cruel and arbitrary power of the adult world. One might think that *Mockingjay*, in which Katniss is finally saved from the Games and delivered to the revolutionary forces to become their figurehead, would offer some redemption, but it turns out the rebels are just as morally ambiguous as Panem's leaders. The full-scale revolution is being sold on television to the disheartened and oppressed Districts, in carefully produced spots with labels like "Because you know who they are and what they do".'

'*Mockingjay* is not as impeccably plotted as *The Hunger Games*, but nonetheless retains its fierce, chilly fascination. At its best the trilogy channels the political passion of *1984*, the memorable violence of *A Clockwork Orange*, the imaginative ambience of *The Chronicles of Narnia* and the detailed inventiveness of *Harry Potter*.

N is for...

Nail Polish

Vanity is a big aspect of *The Hunger Games*, but, yes, you read that right… nail polish! And we're not just talking about the Merry Land of Oz-style Capitol scene, where Katniss is given a makeover, and preened for life. No, we're talking about Lionsgate's decision to go ahead with a *Hunger Games* nail polish line. With a range of colours inspired by characters and scenes from the movie, like Peeta's baker's son brown lipstick and Katniss's multi-coloured interview dress, the line prompted an angry backlash from fans, who called it tacky and said that a fashion line was not really keeping in check with Katniss' anti-fashion character. Lionsgate then reportedly back-pedalled and cancelled the line, – much to the anger of American International Industries and China Glaze, who filed a $10 million lawsuit against the film studio, despite Lionsgate's claims that nothing had been agreed and that they were just merely discussing a promotional deal.

The lawsuit read: 'Lionsgate attempted to justify its actions by claiming that American had supposedly "leaked" information about the contract to the press. The claim was and is completely untrue – American did not 'leak' any information, and so informed Lionsgate immediately.'

However, there were some fans who were disappointed that they couldn't get their hands on the style line of their favourite story. They were sure to be delighted then, when China Glaze and Lionsgate's differences seemed to get settled, with the nail polish line entitled Capitol Colours, and Elizabeth Banks's Effie Trinket officially selected as 'the face' of the line. The tagline reads: 'What Will You Be Wearing to the Opening Ceremonies?' The colours seemed to be the same as the previous range, but they now had different names.

A press release from Lionsgate stated: 'Lionsgate announces that it has partnered with worldwide beauty brand China Glaze on a collection of nail polish to debut in conjunction with the 23 March 2012 release *The Hunger Games*. In keeping with the powerful themes and messages of the story, the collection of nail polish will be inspired exclusively by one of the book's distinct settings – the Capitol of the nation of Panem. Awash in lavish fashion, food, and entertainment, Capitol citizens enjoy extreme cosmetics and body modifications, bold wigs, and outlandish costumes.'

Michelle Andreani from *The Hunger Games* fansite, *TheHob*, said: 'I'll admit to being a little confused at first. It did seem to feed into the book's criticism of superficiality and elitism, and after reading about Katniss struggling in District 12, it's hard to find the Capitol's luxury, well, luxurious. But that doesn't make the Capitol's citizens, and especially their fashion, any less intriguing. And taking a deeper look into that world is sure to be very cool. So, as the marketing campaign starts unfolding, I'm totally on board. After all, you can look great and still have heart. Cinna and Effie prove that much, right?'

O is for...

Overland and Underland

Suzanne Collins was making a successful career in TV when she met children's author James Proimos, who convinced her that she should try giving children's books a go. She was a huge fan of Lewis Carroll's *Alice in Wonderland*, but wondered how today's urban generation would make of the book and its wide open spaces. She reasoned that urban children were more likely to fall down a manhole than a rabbit hole, and that was the germ of the idea for *Gregor the Overlander* and the subsequent four sequels. The series is based around a boy named Gregor, who stumbles upon an underground world in New York, a fantasy land filled with giant rats and cockroaches. Collins said about setting the idea under New York: 'I like the fact that, of all the places Gregor could have travelled to, why the Underland? I liked that this world was teeming under New York City and nobody was aware of it. That you could be going along preoccupied with your own problems and then whoosh! You take a wrong turn in your laundry room and suddenly a giant cockroach is right in your face. No magic, no space or time travel, there's just a ticket to another world behind your clothes dryer.'

Publishers Weekly raved about the first book in the series: 'Collins does a grand job of world-building, with a fine economy of words… Unlike Gregor, who cannot wait to leave, readers will likely find the Underland to be a fantastically engaging place.'

Despite the book's success, Collins admits, after working on scripts for years, that she struggled to adapt to writing a novel rather than TV work. She recalled: 'I think I started the first Gregor book, *Gregor the Overlander*, when I was 38. I'd be clicking along through dialogue and action sequences. That's fine, that's like stage directions. But whenever I hit a descriptive passage, it was like running into a wall. I remember particularly there's a moment early on when Gregor walks through this curtain of moths, and he gets his first look at the underground city of Regalia. So it's this descriptive scene of the city. Wow, did that take me a long time to write! And I went back and looked at it. It's just a couple of paragraphs. It killed me. It took forever.'

She also spent hours on the phone with her military father, desperate for a strategic viewpoint. She reasoned: 'We had two superpowers, the humans and the bats, but the humans were dependent on the alliance with the bats, because then they became aerial fighters.'

P is for...

Pranks

It may be a serious movie they are making, but that didn't stop Josh Hutcherson from having fun in the movie. 'I took a dummy, one that the tracker-jackers were supposed to have attacked, and I put it in Jennifer's bathroom,' Hutcherson told *New York Magazine*'s *Vulture*. 'When she opened the door, she peed her pants. Or so she told me later… I did not get visual confirmation on that one.'

But *The Hunger Games* isn't the only film where you saw the japester at work. 'On *Journey* I had this running prank going when we were shooting in the jungle, where I would take a stick, or a twig, and poke it in someone's ear and make them think they had bugs crawling in there,' he said. 'Vanessa Hudgens and I were messing with Luis Guzman for about eight minutes once, poking something in his ear, pulling it out, watching him freak out. It was so hard not to laugh. And finally he went: "I see you". That was the best one for sure. I think I'm basically a five year old at heart.'

However, one *Journey* co-star that was missing from Hutcherson's pranks was former wrestling superstar, Dwayne Johnson. 'Usually, no one's too big for me to try to take them down – except Dwayne. He gets a free pass. He's huge! Have you seen his pecs? He can sure pop those pecks.'

And Hutcherson wasn't the only prankster on set of *The Hunger Games*. Alexander Ludwig, who plays Cato, recalled: 'One day I was totally sweaty and exhausted after a day of fighting, and I walked into my trailer. I'd already taken off my costume, so I was just in my briefs, and I couldn't find my clothes anywhere! Amandla Stenberg, who plays Rue, and Jackie Emerson, who plays Foxface, had hidden them in the fridge!'

Production

Back in 2009, fans of *The Hunger Games* were delighted when the following press release was sent:

On 17 March, Lionsgate, the leading next generation studio, announced that it has acquired worldwide distribution rights to the film version of Suzanne Collins's best-selling futuristic young adult novel *The Hunger Games*. Collins will adapt the screenplay from her novel, the first in a trilogy. Nina Jacobson is producing through her Color Force shingle. The announcement was made by Joe Drake, Lionsgate President, Motion Picture Group, and Co-Chief Operating Officer.

The Hunger Games was published by Scholastic last year, and has been singled out for raves by *Twilight* author Stephenie Meyer. The trilogy's eagerly anticipated second instalment, *Catching Fire,* is due out on 1 September 2009.

Lionsgate President of Motion Picture Production, Alli Shearmur, will oversee the production for the studio, along with Lionsgate Senior Vice President of Motion Picture Production, Jim Miller.

Said Shearmur: '*The Hunger Games* is an incredible property and it is a thrill to bring it home to Lionsgate. This is exactly the kind of movie I came to Lionsgate to make: youthful, exciting, smart and edgy. We are looking forward to working with Nina and Suzanne to create a movie that satisfies audiences' hunger for high-quality entertainment.

Said Jacobson: 'I am thrilled to have Lionsgate as a partner in *The Hunger Games*.

The suspense of *The Hunger Games* is heightened by its spirit of moral inquiry, and Suzanne has entrusted Lionsgate and me to bring that moral perspective to the adaptation – a charge we fully intend to honour.

The now-defunct British newspaper *News of the World* spoke for many media outlets when it predicted: 'Suzanne Collins's plot rattles along with plenty of action and suspense. It's only a matter of time before the movie version follows.'

Noting the violence of the book in his review of the first novel in *Entertainment Weekly*, Stephen King wryly remarked 'Let's see the makers of the movie version try to get a PG-13 on this baby.' However, that is exactly what they've done.

Collins helped adapt the novel for the film herself. When asked what the differences were between writing novels and scripts, she answered: 'Time, for starters. When you're adapting a novel into a two-hour movie you can't take everything with you. The story has to be condensed to fit the new form. Then there's the question of how best to take a book told in the first person and present tense and to transform it into a satisfying dramatic experience. In the novel, you never leave Katniss for a second and are privy to all of her thoughts, so you need a way to dramatise her inner world and to make it possible for other characters to exist outside of her company.

'Finally, there's the challenge of how to present the violence while still maintaining a PG-13 rating, so that your core audience can view it. A lot of things are acceptable on a page that wouldn't be on a screen. But how certain moments are depicted will ultimately be in the director's hands.'

Gary Ross said about Collins: 'Yeah, she came down to the set, but we also collaborated on the last draft together. I wrote a draft, and then Suzanne and I got along incredibly well, and did the final draft together. She's wonderful.'

Ross added: 'I think one of the most important things when you adapt a book like this is to give people the same kind of visceral experience they had when they read it. I think the reason everybody felt so strongly about what Suzanne did was that they were with this character, they understood her, they were in her shoes, they were in her head. It was such an intense first-person experience. My job in making a film is first and foremost to reflect that.

'How do we get inside Katniss's head? How do we feel what she's feeling? How do we become her? The first thing that allows you to do that is Jennifer Lawrence, because she's such an unbelievable actor. She has so much depth and power and talent and sophistication and sensitivity and subtlety that she's become Katniss Everdeen synonymously. I hope people feel about Jen and Katniss at the end of this three-book cycle the way they feel about Daniel Radcliffe and Harry Potter – that they've become very, synonymous with one another.'

Filming was tough in the North Carolina forest, with Ross saying: 'It was like shooting in Vietnam. I felt like I was making *Apocalypse Now*. The thing was so rigorous. We spent something like six weeks outside in the jungle every day, hiking up and down mountains with cameras and in the mud and in driving rainstorms. We all felt it, but nobody felt it as much as Jen did. It's been an intense physical experience for her.'

Liam Hemsworth said: 'It was all shot in North

Carolina. It was awesome. We shot in a place called Asheville, which is full of beautiful, beautiful forests. And when we shot all the Reaping scenes, it was just crazy. The Reaping in the book and the script is such an emotional thing and it really did feel like that when we were shooting it. You know, the thought of young kids going off into this scary kind of world was pretty crazy.'

Amandla Stenberg said the cast had a ball: 'Definitely! We were going to get sushi every night and going swimming. It was super fun. We all learned from each other. We weren't separated by our ages at all. We just became one big family and I definitely think that all the older actors and actresses that I worked with really became my role models – and also kind of like my big brother and sister figures, too.'

On 15 September 2011, the following press release was announced:

Lionsgate, a leading global entertainment company, today announced the close of principal photography on the highly anticipated film adaptation of Suzanne Collins's runaway bestselling novel *The Hunger Games*. Lionsgate will release *The Hunger Games* on 23 March 2012. The film is the first in a series that Lionsgate is making based on the book trilogy that has become a worldwide phenomenon.

Filmed entirely in North Carolina, the locations spanned from a dense forest, in which the arena that hosts the games themselves was created, to a town that stood in for Katniss's home, District 12, to a sound stage that was the platform for the fantastical sights and sounds of The Capitol, the futuristic capital city of the nation of Panem. Principal photography on the 84-day production began on 23 May 2011.

The film pairs Oscar nominee Jennifer Lawrence (*Winter's Bone, X-Men First Class*) with Josh Hutcherson (*The Kid's Are All Right*) and Liam Hemsworth (*The Last Song*) in the key young adult roles. Rounding out the cast is a Who's Who of acclaimed adult actors: Oscar nominee Woody Harrelson, Elizabeth Banks, Lenny Kravitz, Oscar nominee Stanley Tucci, Donald Sutherland, Wes Bentley and Toby Jones.

'It has been an absolute thrill watching *The Hunger Games*, a project that has truly become part of Lionsgate's DNA since our acquisition of the book in 2009, come to life. What I observed on set was impressive on every level, and reinforced my confidence that we have assembled precisely the right team to bring Suzanne Collins's brilliant novel to the big screen, said Joe Drake, Lionsgate's co-COO and Motion Picture Group President.

Although the intensely anticipated sets were closed to press and visitors, Lionsgate and the filmmakers were able to reach out and touch the incredibly eager fans several times during the production process.

Lionsgate debuted the central cast trio through two *Entertainment Weekly* covers, featuring Jennifer Lawrence in character as Katniss and Josh Hutcherson and Liam Hemsworth in character as Peeta and Gale. It marked the first time that a studio has revealed a principal cast of film characters on sequential national magazine covers.

Winners of The Ultimate Hunger Games Fan Sweeps, a global contest where fans entered to win the opportunity to be flown to the set of *The Hunger Games*, was the one exception to the film's closed-set policy. In mid August, five winners from around the world and their guests got a glimpse of the sets, observed the filming of a scene and met the cast.

A heavily promoted first look at footage from the film debuted on MTV's 2011 Video Music

Awards on 28 August. The show attracted MTV's biggest audience in the network's history, with a record-breaking 12.4 million total viewers.

Parody

You know you've entered into pop culture when you become parodied – step forward *The Hunger Games* spoof *The Hunger but Mainly Death Games: A Parody*, which has received favourable praise from readers.

Here is the blurb: 'Mockstrich season has begun. Welcome to *The Hunger But Mainly Death Games*, the hilarious *Hunger Games* parody, and the only book brave enough to suggest that Suzanne Collins's epic trilogy was way more about death than food. Or at least this is what Bratniss Everclean discovers, when she leaves the comforts of Slum 12, Pandumb's garbage dump, to short-sightedly volunteer for a teenage death tournament. But she soon realises there are fates worse than death…like weirdly having to date her fellow competitor, and lifelong stalker, Pita Malarkey. Okay, okay, it's not worse than death, but it's still pretty annoying. Still, with help from her agent Oofie Triptrip and her mentor, Hagridmitch, who's confident he can guide Bratniss to victory in the Tri-Wizard Cup, maybe

Bratniss will somehow survive this book that she's the narrator of.

'*The Hunger But Mainly Death Games* is the perfect book for anyone who's going through *Hunger Games* withdrawal and ready for a wonderfully twisted take on their favourite story and characters. This book is also for those unfortunate teens who are trapped in a *Hunger Games* at this very moment and could really benefit from some levity. We're here for you, assuming you brought your e-reader into the arena.'

Another one is entitled *The Hunger Pains: A Parody*, from Havard Lampoon, the world's longest continually published humour magazine, which has included content from comedians who have written for *The Simpsons*, *Seinfeld*, *The Office*, *30 Rock* and *Late Night with David Letterman*.

Parodies of best-selling books have become a regular occurrence nowadays, thanks to the success of several *Twilight* parodies.

Peeta Mellark

Peeta Mellark is the male Tribute of District 12 for the 74th *Hunger Games*.

The accustomed pre-match interview saw him confessing his love for District 12's female Tribute,

Katniss. Some might have called it a cynical move designed to win sponsors. However, he has had a crush on her ever since he was five years old, which was cemented when he heard her sing and realised that even the birds stopped to listen. When a young Katniss was left starving and rummaging around the streets for food, Peeta, a baker's son, gave bread to her.

Josh Hutcherson, who plays Peeta, told *Vanity Fair*: 'At times when you're adapting a book into a movie, you have to take certain creative liberties to bridge the gap between the two forms of media. And with Suzanne involved, I feel like that can really ease people's minds who are worried about it being changed too much, because it's staying true to the story.'

'We had a pretty small crew for being such a giant movie, which was really nice also, because when you had these big emotional scenes on set, it's not like there's, you know, 150 people standing there and staring at you. You became really close with everyone, and it was like a little family, which in my opinion made it much more comfortable to give really great performances.'

Q is for...

Jack Quaid

Jack Quaid plays Marvel in *The Hunger Games*. Marvel is described on *TheHungerGames.Wikia.com* as follows: 'Marvel is the male tribute from District 1 in the 74th *Hunger Games*. As a Career Tribute, Marvel is strong and ruthless. It is unknown if he volunteered for the Games or was reaped. He presumably trained for a lot of his pre-Games life, like most Tributes from his District. During the opening ceremonies, he and his District partner Glimmer were spray-painted silver and were wearing tunics. Katniss pointed out that they both looked gorgeous. During training, he showed great skill at spear throwing. He, along with the other Careers, received a training score somewhere between 8 and 10.'

Quaid said about playing Marvel in *Interview Magazine*: 'I do something horrible to someone very small and cute, and then I have my ass handed to me immediately after.' The 19 year old was told upon landing the part to expect people to spit on him on the streets.

It's his feature film debut after only working on short films with friends – most notably *The Invasion of the Douchebags*, which features a plot comprising of a Phil Collins track triggering the residents of Martha's Vineyards into idiots. 'One was filmed with a budget of millions of dollars, and the other was filmed with a budget of about 20 bucks – which went towards the sunglasses I wore in it,' he said.

Currently studying in the Experimental Theatre Wing at New York University, Quaid said: 'I've been on sets my whole life. But this is the first time in front of the camera and not in a chair with a packet of Sour Patch Kids from the craft services truck. It was a new sensation. It was weird... I really liked it.'

Quaid is the son of Hollywood actors Dennis Quaid and Meg Ryan, who married in 1991 and had Jack a year later. Sadly they divorced in 2001, and in a 2008 interview, Ryan said: 'Dennis was not faithful to me for a very long time, and that was very painful. I found out more about that after I was divorced.'

Dennis Quaid hit back, saying: 'It was eight years ago, and I find it unbelievable that Meg continues to rehash and rewrite the story of our relationship. Also, I find it regrettable that our son, Jack, has to be reminded in a public way of the turmoil and pain that every child feels in a divorce.

I, myself, moved on years ago and am fortunate to have a happy, beautiful family.'

R is for...

Reality TV

While *The Hunger Games* features a lot of inspiration based on classic culture, Collins cites the modern phenomenon of the reality show as another huge influence. In fact, it was watching reality TV that kick-started an idea in Collins's brain that would eventually transform into the much-loved novel. She said: 'The Games are televised across the country of Panem and it is mandatory to watch them, because they are not only supposed to be entertainment, but of course they are a reminder that the Districts are punished for having the audacity to rebel against the Capitol.'

When asked why reality TV is such a phenomenon at the moment, Collins replied: 'Well, they're often set up as games and, like sporting events, there's an interest in seeing who wins. The contestants are usually unknown, which makes them relatable. Sometimes they have very talented people performing. Then there's the voyeuristic thrill – watching people being humiliated, or brought to tears, or suffering physically – which I find very disturbing. There's also the potential for desensitizing the audience, so that when they see real tragedy playing out on, say, the news, it doesn't have the impact it should.'

Jennifer Lawrence said: 'I love that *The Hunger Games* is kind of this sick look at our world that's obsessed with reality TV and brutality. We've become so numb to the shock factor. We see people die on TV now, we see dead bodies and blood on the nightly news. I mean, the things people can find on YouTube are crazy! We're so desperate to it all now. Also, there's the message of history repeating itself. There are these scenes where it honestly looks like Gladiators fighting. Roman history, with people murdering other people for nothing more than entertainment, I just think all of that is hard-hitting and fascinating.'

Real Life Hunger Games

Yes, the series isn't real and there isn't really a society where they kill youngsters. But one school in Niagara, Ontario, in the US, saw 700 students participate in their own week-long version.

Cheryl Caldwell, a literacy consultant for the District School Board of Niagara, told *The Standard*: 'We wanted to make it living literature. Even kids who have given up on reading are getting right into these books. A lot of the kids were saying: "*Lord of the Flies*, my parents read that." We thought that maybe it was time to look at something else, something they read.'

Students teamed up to build shelters, while some hunted for food and supplies. If they were caught by another student, they can surrender their supplies, negotiate or fight, which consisted of rock, paper, scissors.

'There is an emphasis on compromise, which is very similar to the novel. You have to deal with people that you don't know. Alliances are a big thing in the books and we're kind of doing that, we're working with people we don't know at all,' she said.

Recipes

The Hunger Games fans and budding chefs have come

together to make a series of recipes, which are based on food in the movies, including District 11's Crescent Moon rolls. Here is the recipe for Katniss's favourite lamb stew with dried plums, as published on *FictionalFood.net*:

Ingredients:
- 3 lbs lamb meat, cubed
- 2-3 tbsp cooking oil
- 1 tbsp sugar
- 3 tbsp flour
- 2 cans beef broth
- 1 cup tomato pulp or 3 tbsp tomato paste
- 1 sprig rosemary, leaves snipped
- Salt and pepper to taste
- 3 large carrots, peeled and chopped
- 2 medium potatoes, peeled and chopped
- 16-18 pearl onions, peeled and halved
- 1 cup frozen or fresh peas
- 1 handful dried plums cut in half

Instructions:
1. Heat oven to 475 degrees.
2. Heat oil in a skillet and brown lamb meat. Transfer to ovenproof dish as pieces cook.
3. Sprinkle sugar on browned meat. Cook meat

for several minutes on medium high heat to caramelize sugar.

4. Toss meat with flour until well coated. Place pot in oven uncovered for 5 minutes. Toss meat around and cook for another 5 minutes. Reduce oven heat to 350 degrees.

5. Add 1 1/2 cans of beef broth, tomato pulp, and rosemary. Cover and cook on bottom third of the oven for 1 hour.

6. Taste and season with salt and pepper as needed. Add carrots, onions, and potatoes and more broth if needed.

7. Cover and return pot to oven for another hour. After 30 minutes, add dried plums. Once done, taste and season as needed.

8. On the stovetop, boil peas for 1-2 minutes. Drain and add to stew just before serving.

9. Serve on wild rice. Eat by the bucketful.

Other recipes can be found in Emily Ansara Baines's book *The Unofficial Hunger Games Cookbook: From Lamb Stew to Groosling – More than 150 recipes inspired by The Hunger Games trilogy*.

The *Wall Street Journal* wrote: 'In the post-apocalyptic fantasy series *The Hunger Games*, starving characters eat whatever they can kill or forage: wild dog, horse, tree bark, mouse meat... fans have become obsessed with the food in the books, trying home preparation of dishes such as fire-roasted rabbit and seaweed bread. This month, *The Unofficial Hunger Games Cookbook* was published, with 150 recipes for rustic, gamy fare including fried squirrel and raccoon in bacon drippings, though none for dog. Food, and the lack of it, is a recurring theme in the dystopian trilogy.'

Red Dawn

Red Dawn is based on the 1984 cult hit, and tells of a group of teenagers trying to fend off a foreign invasion on American soil. The invaders were Russian in the original, with the remake using Chinese soldiers, before being edited to make it look like a North Korean invaders in post production.

The reason for the remake was simple, according to the film's screenwriter: 'The tone is going to be very intense, very much keeping in mind the post-9/11 world that we're in. As *Red Dawn* scared the heck out of people in 1984, we feel that the world is kind of already filled with a lot of paranoia and unease, so why not scare the hell out of people again?'

However, the film's original director and writer,

John Milius, disagreed, ranting: 'I think it's a stupid thing to do. The movie is not very old.' Milius, who wasn't involved in the new film, but was given a chance to read the script, said: 'It was terrible. There was a strange feeling to the whole thing. They were fans of the movie, so they put in stuff they thought was neat. It's all about neat action scenes and has nothing to do with the story. There's only one example in 4,000 years of Chinese territorial adventurism, and that was in 1979, when they invaded Vietnam, and to put it mildly they got their butts handed to them. Would China want us? They sell us stuff. We're a market. I would have done it about Mexico.'

It wasn't just Milius who disagreed about the invaders, and despite post-production costs equalling a reported million dollars, they were changed to North Koreans.

Starring Josh Hutcherson and Liam Hemsworth's brother, Chris, filming began in 2009. Chris Hemsworth said about the changes: 'It was always pretty vague, even when we were shooting. They kind of never mentioned who the invaders were anyway. It wasn't heavily suggested, so I think it was an easy technical fix for them whether they do it with a little CGI or the occasional voiceover line. It wasn't really a political take on anything. It could've been the

Australians for all we cared. I guess MGM have their reasons for doing it, but we as the actors were never really involved with it.'

Producer Tripp Vinson added: 'This movie has been rebooted because the filmmakers all love the original movie. The experience of seeing *Red Dawn* as a young boy in the middle of a Cold War, was life changing for me, and a whole generation. I assure you that everyone involved with the reboot is keenly aware of the responsibility of delivering a movie that can stand eye to eye with the original.

'The changes made to *Red Dawn* were made in consultation with military think-tanks and people that specialise in game theory. Really smart people who spend their days constructing doomsday scenarios for our military and government. The type of people who can project a series of events that could lead to some very scary things happening to our country. I can assure you, we listened a lot to those people, especially with regards to the capability of the North Korean military.'

He added: '*Red Dawn* isn't for everyone. So, if you are interested in seeing a movie filled with preachy political discussions, *Red Dawn* ain't for you. If you love movies in which Americans are the bad guys, *Red Dawn* ain't for you. If you get emotional watching daytime television, *Red Dawn* ain't for you. If you're a vegetarian, *Red Dawn* probably ain't for you. But, if you like meat with your potatoes, muscle cars that roar, tanks, guns and things blowing the f**kup by Americans kicking some Commie ass – then we have something special coming your way.'

There were high hopes for the movie, but those were initially dashed in 2010 because of the financial problems surrounding its studio, MGM. However, the film is expected to be released later in 2012.

Josh Hutcherson said '*Red Dawn* was great. It's like playing pretend, being a little kid doing these movies. When I was a little kid I'd play army... so I was just playing army, as far as I was concerned. They gave me real guns, which was scary and exciting. But I'm really excited for it to come out finally.'

He added: 'My character's name is Robert and he kind of starts off as this sort of quieter, almost borderline nerd guy, and then by the end, after the invasion, he just sort of loses it and starts really kicking butt. So it's pretty awesome. One of my favourite things to do in a film is take a character from A to B.'

S is for...

Suzanne Collins

In 2008, the world was in love with a pair of star crossed supernatural lovers – Edward Cullen and Bella Swan. The *Twilight* craze had sunk its teeth into the publishing and film world. Everyone wanted a bite of this phenomenon and soon you couldn't move past bookshelves, TV channels and DVD aisles without seeing authors and directors trying to create their own horror romance franchise. Some stuck to the vampire theme, while others tried their hands at other mythical creatures like werewolves and zombies. It was clear that for the time being if you wanted a mega hit you needed romance, angst and a creature that went bump in the night.

Indeed, that year there was one young adult novel that was on everyone's radar – Stephenie Meyer's final *Twilight* instalment, *Breaking Dawn*. There were 3.2 million first prints of the book available, compared to *The Hunger Games* modest 50,000 copies.

However, there was rising expectancy for Collins's book *The Hunger Games,* following early rave reviews from bloggers.

As a young child Collins lived in Brussels, Belgium. She went to an American school there but learnt French and Flemish. She said although she doesn't know much Flemish, one phrase she remembers vividly is 'It's forbidden to climb up on the tank'… and one time she did climb up onto a tank, to get a better view of the North Sea, but was promptly told off.

Her childhood was one fraught with worry. Unsurprising, considering her dad was stationed in Vietnam during the war. She said: 'My father was in the Air Force for some 30 years. He was also a Vietnam veteran, he was there the year I was six. Beyond that, though, he was a doctor of political science, a military specialist, and a historian – he was a very intelligent man. And he felt that it was part of his responsibility to teach us, his children, about history and war. When I think back, at the centre of all this is the question of what makes a necessary war – at what point is it justifiable or unavoidable?'

If Collins's series *The Underland Chronicles* featured some military strategy, with the help of her dad, *The Hunger Games* was a more apt tribute to him – showcasing the horror and devastation conflicts can cause.

While she had plenty to draw on, it was in fact reality TV that we have to thank for the *Hunger Games* series. Collins had the television on, flicking through the channels absent-mindedly. A blur of visuals flicked through her mind as she tried to figure out a good programme to watch. A reality show came on, and then on another channel she saw footage of the Iraq war. Instantly, something clicked in her head. Without realising she had formed the seed of an idea for the book.

'I was channel surfing between reality TV programmes and actual war coverage. On one channel, there's a group of young people competing for I don't even know what, and on the next, there's a group of young people fighting in an actual war. I was really tired, and the lines between these stories started to blur in a very unsettling way. That's the moment when Katniss's story came to me,' she said.

Her book editor Kate Egan said: 'I was doing the final edits on the last Gregor book, when my second child was born. It was a month before I was ready to get back to editing. Suzanne used that time to write the proposal for *The Hunger Games* trilogy. The original proposal had the fight to the death and the intriguing character of Katniss. I realised that this was going to be the biggest book I'd ever worked on.

'Storytelling is Suzanne's strength. As an editor, I help her develop the characters. For example, I asked her for more of the Peeta-Katniss-Gale love triangle. Suzanne was more focused on the war story. We've learned to trust each other. Sometimes Suzanne thinks it's obvious where she is going, but I tell her I don't see it. When I need help following, it's a sign that the manuscript needs some shoring up.'

She has a unique writing structure. Collins explained in a past interview: 'Each of the books has 27 chapters divided into nine sections. And that probably comes from my play-writing background, during a time in my life when I wrote three-act plays; it's a very comfortable structure for me to use. At the end of each nine chapters, a new part begins, and I call them act breaks like you would in play-writing – because that is how I think of them.'

Delving into wilderness survival books as research,

she also had help from her dad's stories growing up, explaining: 'He grew up during the Great Depression. For his family, hunting was not a sport but a way to put meat on the table. He also knew a certain amount about edible plants. He'd go into the woods and gather all these wild mushrooms and bring them home and sauté them. My mom wouldn't let any of us go near them! But he'd eat them up and they never harmed him, so I guess he knew which ones were safe, because wild mushrooms can be very deadly. I also read a big stack of wilderness survival guide books. And here's what I learned: You've got to be really good to survive out there for more than a few days.'

One of the more unsettling aspects of the book involves the killing of children, and Collins knows that the death of her characters and the killings of young people make it hard for her to write. However, conceding that it was painful and difficult to write those scenes she is committed to tell the story and these things happen in her universe. And if you can't do it, maybe tell another story.

Collins said: 'You have to accept from the beginning that you're going to kill characters. It's a horrible thing to do, and it's a horrible thing to write, particularly when you have to take out a character that is vulnerable or young or someone you've grown to love while you were writing about them. Given that, you have to remember who you're trying to reach with the book. I try and think of how I would tell a particularly difficult event to my own children. Exactly what details they need to know how to really understand it, and what would be gratuitous.'

However, when things got too heavy she would lighten the mood by freelancing for a Nick Jr. show called *Wow! Wow! Wubbzy!* She had begun her career writing children's TV, and when things got too dark working on the book, heading to *Wow! Wow! Wubbzy!* was a welcome relief!

'I adore it,' she said in an interview. 'It's a very fun preschool show that's set in the imaginary town called Wuzzleburg. When I was working on *The Hunger Games* – there's not a lot of levity in it – I'd do a *Wubbzy* script. It's an enormous relief to spend some hours in Wuzzleburg, writing an 11-minute episode, where I know things are going to work out just fine and all the characters will be alive at the end of the programme.'

Collins has stated that she always had plans for the *Hunger Games* trilogy. 'While I didn't know every detail, of course, the arc of the story from Gladiator games, to revolution, to war, to the eventual outcome, remained constant throughout the writing process,' she explained.

Stephenie Meyer

Twilight came to Stephenie Meyer in a dream. 'I had a dream about a vampire and a woman talking in a meadow. It came from nowhere. It sounds cheesy but it was a great dream. And once I started I didn't need another dream. The story wrote itself,' said Meyer, in the *Twilight* DVD documentary *A Conversation With Stephenie Meyer.*

She added: '2 June 2003, I know the exact day that I woke up from the dream and started writing. The meadow scene in the movie is basically the dream that I had. I wanted to know what happened to those characters. I was so afraid that I would forget this great dream that I wrote 10 pages, pretty much the whole of chapter 13, and then after that I just wanted to know what happened. I didn't expect to write a novel – it was just a chance to play with the characters in my head. When I finished it no one was more shocked than me to see I had finished a book!'

Twilight is told from the perspective of Bella, a 17-year-old teenager who is forced to move from her mother's home of sunny Scottsdale to her father's rain-drenched world in the small town of Forks.

After enrolling and making a small group of friends, she is intrigued by the Cullen clan – a group of impossibly attractive boys and girls. Then Edward appears. Constantly described as the most beautiful person ever, the pair embark on a passionate, dramatic and dangerous romance.

The result of Meyer's dream went on to become a massive success, reaching number five on *The New York Times* best-seller list and spawning three other books in the series – *New Moon, Eclipse* and *Breaking Dawn*. The four books have sold over 25 million copies worldwide.

The Hunger Games as seen as its spiritual successor, both featuring heart-rending love between three characters set against a thrilling backdrop of adventure. Not that Stephenie Meyer sees *The Hunger Games* as competition. She praised the book on her website, raving: 'People often ask me for reading suggestions, and I'm always happy to share because books are exciting things to me. My latest excitement is this: *The Hunger Games* by Suzanne Collins. I was so obsessed with this book I had to take it with me out to dinner and hide it under the edge of the table so I wouldn't have to stop reading. The story kept me up for several nights in a row, because even after I was finished, I just lay in bed wide awake thinking about it. I've been recommending it to total strangers in Target. And now to everyone who reads my website. *The Hunger Games* is amazing.'

And she was just as fulsome with the praise when discussing *Catching Fire* – raving: 'I got an early look at a book I've been eagerly awaiting: *Catching Fire*, the sequel to Suzanne Collins's phenomenal *The Hunger Games*. It not only lived up to my high expectations, it surpassed them. It's just as exciting as *The Hunger Games*, but even more gut-wrenching, because you already know these characters, you've already suffered with them. Suzanne takes the story to places I wasn't expecting, and she's never afraid to take it to very hard places. Stunning. You won't sleep when you're reading this one.'

Despite the comparisons to *Twilight*, Josh Hutcherson distanced *The Hunger Games* from it: 'I think it's unfair because it gives really big expectations for what we're supposed to do at the box office. The *Twilight* movies are ridiculously successful. As far as the stories go they're both very different. There are some similarities, with it being a popular younger teen book and there being a bit of love, but in *Twilight* it's about vampires and werewolves, in our world it's a futuristic world that's very realistic. It's about survival and giving power to the people.'

Stephen Soderbergh

Befitting the quality of the Collins's book, the film version of *The Hunger Games* is packed with some of cinema's biggest talents, both upcoming and established, like veterans Woody Harrelson and Elizabeth Banks and rising stars Liam Hemsworth, Jennifer Lawrence and Josh Hutcherson. However, the film also boasts an excellent crew member, with acclaimed Oscar-winning director Steven Soderbergh taking on second unit directing duties. These are generally seen as one of the jobs that fledgling directors do before they take the step up, where they usually pick up shots not involving the main cast. The rumour about Soderbergh first started in August 2011, with the film's production designer Eddie Mills tweeting: 'Soderbergh's in the house this weekend,' and electrician Chrys Blackstone, adding: 'Holy s**t! Just found out that Steven Soderbergh is coming to the #hungergames to direct 2nd Unit. I am so excited, this is getting good!'

Soderbergh has been friends with Gary Ross for years, with Soderbergh producing Ross's *Pleasantville* movie, and Ross often looks over Soderbergh's scripts. There is another connection, in that the film's production designer, Phil Messina, is a regular on Soderbergh's films. Apparently Ross simply asked his friend and he said yes.

Another bonus is Soderbergh's pace. He works fast. When shooting *Contagion*, cast member Matt Damon wowed: 'Steven would have his headphones on, sitting at his laptop. And in about 20 minutes he'd cut together the day's work. "OK," he'd say, then pull his headphones off and turn the computer around and show us, right there, what we'd shot that day and how it would look on the big screen when the movie comes out. That fast. He's a FREAK!'

Soderbergh couldn't believe the fuss his appearance on *The Hunger Games* set made, telling *Movie Fone*: 'I show up in North Carolina, a crew member Tweets: "Steven Soderbergh's here." And immediately the f*cking firestorm starts. Why is he here? What's going on? Is the movie in trouble? Is he directing footage from the second one?... all of this crazy-ass speculation, with people just spinning off.

'The story is really simple. Back in April, when Gary – who is a close friend of mine I've exchanged creative favours with non-stop over the last 15 years – got the boards for the shoot in April, he called me and said: "Hey, first week of August, I got these two days of second unit. Is there any way you can come down and help me out? Because I'd rather have you do it than hire somebody who I don't know." I said: "Actually, that works out; we'll just be finishing *Contagion* and prepping *Magic Mike* and, yeah, it could be fun."

'Cut to two months later, and I show up to do this thing. What's fun about it, for me, is that my job is to come in and duplicate exactly what Gary and Tom Stern, the [cinematographer], are doing. To mimic their aesthetic as closely as I can. And that's what I attempted to do. But if I've done my job properly, I hope I did, by design, you won't be able to tell what I did. Because it's supposed to cut seamlessly into what they're doing. That's the whole point. That's why he asked me to come down, because he knew that I would be rigorous about matching what they were doing.'

Ironically enough, the esteemed film director actually felt nervous in his new and strange role, adding: 'Gary showed me stuff on either side of the area in which I was going to be shooting stuff and we talked at length. And I thought,: "okay I see what you guys are doing. I know what the tool kit is and what the rules are." And it was fun, in a way. But I found it much more nerve-wracking than when you're shooting for yourself, because I was constantly thinking, "Oh, I hope that he likes this. I hope he likes that…" I was really back to that situation of being the person who has to please someone else – as opposed to pleasing myself. And that made me really anxious. You know, I wanted to do a good job... Gary is a friend of mine.'

Stephen King

The Hunger Games book wasn't just a hit with normal book fans, it had other authors raving, too, including *Twilight's* Stephenie Meyer and horror writing legend Stephen King. King praised it for being really addictive in his review for *Entertainment Weekly*, but claimed that it displayed 'authorial laziness that kids will accept more readily than adults'. He also noted that the reality TV format was used in *Battle Royale* and *The Running Man* – a novella that King wrote under his alias Richard Backman. He raved:

'As negative Utopias go, Suzanne Collins has created a dilly. The United States is gone. North America has become Panem, a TV-dominated dictatorship run from a city called the Capitol. The rest of Panem is divided into 12 Districts (the former 13th had the bad judgement to revolt and no longer exists). The yearly highlight in this nightmare world is *The Hunger Games*, a bloodthirsty reality TV show in which 24 teenagers chosen by lottery – two from each District

– fight each other in a desolate environment called the "arena." The winner gets a life of ease; the losers get death. The only unspoken rule is that you can't eat the dead contestants. Let's see the makers of the movie version try to get a PG-13 on this baby.

'Our heroine is Katniss Everdeen (lame name, cool kid), a resident of District 12, which used to be Appalachia. She lives in a desperately poor mining community called the Seam, and when her little sister's name is chosen as one of the contestants in the upcoming *Hunger Games*, Katniss volunteers to take her place. A gutsy decision, given the fact that District 12 hasn't produced a *Hunger Games* winner in 30 years or so, making it the Chicago Cubs of the post-apocalypse world. Complicating Katniss's already desperate situation is her growing affection for the other District 12 contestant, a clueless baker's son named Peeta Mellark. Further complicating her situation is her sorta-crush on her 18-year-old hunting partner, Gale. Gale isn't clueless; Gale is smouldering. Says so right on page 14.

'The love triangle is fairly standard teen-read stuff; what 16-year-old girl wouldn't like to have two interesting guys to choose from? The rest of *The Hunger Games*, however, is a violent, jarring speed-rap of a novel that generates nearly constant suspense and may also generate a fair amount of controversy. I couldn't stop reading, and once I got over the main character's name (Gale calls her Catnip – ugh), I got to like her a lot. And although "young adult novel" is a dumbbell term I put right up there with "jumbo shrimp" and "airline food" in the oxymoron sweepstakes, how many novels so categorised feature one character stung to death by monster wasps and another more or less eaten alive by mutant werewolves? I say more or less because Katniss, a bow-and-arrow Annie Oakley, puts the poor kid out of his misery before the werewolves can get to the prime cuts.

'Collins is an efficient no-nonsense prose stylist with a pleasantly dry sense of humour. Reading *The Hunger Games* is as addictive (and as violently simple) as playing one of those shoot-it-if-it-moves videogames in the lobby of the local eightplex; you know it's not real, but you keep plugging in quarters anyway. Balancing off the efficiency are displays of authorial laziness that kids will accept more readily than adults. When Katniss needs burn cream or medicine for Peeta, whom she more or less babysits during the second half of the book, the stuff floats down from the sky on silver parachutes. And although the bloody action in the arena is televised by multiple cameras, Collins never mentions Katniss seeing one. Also, readers of *Battle*

Royale (by Koushun Takami), *The Running Man*, or *The Long Walk* (those latter two by some guy named Bachman) will quickly realise they have visited these TV badlands before. But since this is the first novel of a projected trilogy, it seems to me that the essential question is whether or not readers will care enough to stick around and find out what comes next for Katniss. I know I will. But then, I also have a habit of playing *Time Crisis* until all my quarters are gone.'

T is for...

Theseus

Suzanne Collins has already admitted that it was reality shows that first brought the idea of *The Hunger Games* to her, but it was the Greek myths that formed the basic plot of the film. She is obsessed with Greek myths, and one of her favourite ones is about Theseus. The myth sees the city of Athens forced to send young men and women to Crete to be devoured by the mighty Minotaur. She said: 'Crete was sending a very clear message: mess with us and we'll do something worse than kill you. We'll kill your children'.

Collins has already admitted that Katniss is a

futuristic Theseus. She explains: 'It's very much based on the myth of Theseus and the Minotaur, which I read when I was eight. I was a huge fan of Greek and Roman mythology. As punishment for displeasing Crete, Athens periodically had to send seven youths and seven maidens to Crete, where they were thrown into the labyrinth and devoured by the Minotaur, a monster that's half man and half bull. Even when I was a little kid, the story took my breath away, because it was so cruel, and Crete was so ruthless, and the parents sat by apparently powerless to stop it. The cycle doesn't end until Theseus volunteers to go, and he kills the Minotaur. In her own way, Katniss is a futuristic Theseus. But I didn't want to do a labyrinth story. So I decided to write basically an updated version of the Roman Gladiator games.'

She added: 'In keeping with the classical roots, I send my Tributes into an updated version of the Roman Gladiator games, which entails a ruthless government forcing people to fight to the death as popular entertainment. The world of Panem, particularly the Capitol, is loaded with Roman references. Panem itself comes from the expression "Panem et Circenses", which translates into "Bread and Circuses". The audiences for both the Roman games and reality TV are almost characters in themselves. They can respond with great enthusiasm or play a role in your elimination.'

The Kids Are All Right

If *Winter's Bone* was Jennifer Lawrence's calling card to Hollywood bosses, *The Kids Are All Right* was Josh Hutcherson's. The ensemble-led drama is an astute and keenly aware piece about the conflicts and tensions that can arise in a modern family.

The production notes stated the synopsis as thus: 'In this funny, vibrant, and richly drawn portrait of a modern family, Nic and Jules (Annette Bening and Julianne Moore) are two mothers who share a cozy suburban craftsman bungalow with their respective teenage children, Joni and Laser (Mia Wasikowska and Josh Hutcherson). As Joni prepares to leave for college, her younger brother presses her for a big favour. He wants Joni, now 18, to help him find their biological father. Against her better judgement, Joni honours her brother's request and manages to make contact with 'bio-dad' Paul (Mark Ruffalo), an easy-going restaurateur. As Paul comes into the lives of this straight-shooting family, an unexpected new chapter begins for the group as family ties are defined, re-defined, and then re-re-defined.'

'The script was incredible,' Hutcherson said. 'It was unlike anything that I had read before. It was such a full adaptation of what a family means. I think that the characters are so well written and the dialogue was so incredibly realistic that I knew that I wanted to be a part of it.

'I met with Lisa Cholodenko, the director. I'd been a fan of hers for a while from *Laurel Canyon*, and I think she did an amazing job with writing it, directing it, and everything and just to be part of the film was an honour and it was awesome.'

He also added: 'It's actually a very similar dynamic to my family. We're very, very close, not only as a family, but as friends. I practically am with my mum 24/7 because she's been on set with me since I was nine years old and so, I'm around her a lot. I just feel like I have a good friendship with my family. I think that's very important because Laser's family has a very strong mutual respect for one another. Laser definitely does things sometimes and needs some parenting.'

He added: 'A lot of it was the writing. Lisa and Stuart did a great job of capturing these characters and the essence of who they were. They worked on it for almost five years. For me I just played the part that was on the page. Laser is a teen who's trying to figure out who he is and how he fits into the world, and I know I identified with that. I'm pretty sure that most teenagers out there, and adults who have ever been teenagers, can identify with that as well.'

Mark Ruffalo said about agreeing to appear in the movie: 'I'd just directed my film and was in post when I got the call for this film. It didn't look like it was going to work out with my schedule to do this. I was literally shooting when I had to deliver my movie and I had been away from my family. It was a tough year. So, I was thinking I needed a break. They couldn't move their dates around, so it sort of looked like it wasn't going to happen, which was really heart-breaking to me. I was telling my wife about it all the time. In fact, finally she was texting [Julianne Moore] – they're friends – and she said: "What's up with that movie? I love that movie. Mark loved that movie. What's going on with it?". They said the part was still open and asked if I would do it and my wife said: "Yeah, he won't talk about anything else." So it kind of all came together.'

Ruffalo added: 'I thought it was a really interesting turn on kind of an American iconic life character – a kind of Peter Pan bachelor who lives his life purely for his own pleasure. A lot of us have looked up to people like that and wanted to be one. Then he has this really nice turn in it, when he meets his biological kids. They make him a pile of mush.'

Julianne Moore said: 'The whole cast is tremendous, and it's the strength of the script that attracted them to *The Kids Are All Right*. I first met Lisa years ago at a Women In Film event. I'd seen *High Art*, and thought it was brilliant. I actually said to her: "Why didn't I see that script?!" I think she's a wonderful writer and director, and we stayed in touch and were looking for things to do. She sent me the script that she and Stuart had written, I said yes, and then it was a long process of actually bringing the film to fruition. I stuck with it because I believed in Lisa as a filmmaker, and I believed in the beautiful script as a movie.'

Stuart Blumberg said: 'Mia Wasikowska may seem to be one of those "it girls" who's exploded onto the scene, but she's incredibly level-headed and calm. She brought a real centeredness to playing Joni, a real gravitas to this 18 year old. Josh Hutcherson did a wonderful job; he's not at all like Laser in real life. We'd see him go from his own extroverted self to playing someone very internal and almost imploding.'

While the script appealed to Hutcherson, he was carving out a successful mainstream career. This was indie fare, and several of those films, however acclaimed, get rarely seen. But Hutcherson is canny enough to know that if he wants a fulfilling career he needs to grow as an actor.

'Ever since I first started acting I've wanted to have a long career,' he explained. 'This is just a step in the direction of becoming more of an adult actor. The story was so real and it encapsulated the family and depicted it in a way that has never been done before, and it definitely is a genre and a type of movie I haven't been in before, and I loved it. As an actor, I feel like a lot of times your job is to portray real life or the complete opposite, a fantastical world. I've done a lot of fantastical crazy stuff that doesn't exist, so to break it down into something that was so real and genuine and fun like this was really fun and different.'

When asked about the differences between this and his usual fare, he replied: 'It's very different. *Zathura* was a 93-day shoot, and this was 23. I loved it. The intimacy that you get with an independent film like this is unlike a studio film. The collaboration and the creative freedom that you have is really nice. I love doing giant studio pictures, they're a lot of fun, big budgets and a lot of action and long shoots. But I also love breaking it down and doing character pieces – it sounds really actor-y to call them pieces, but I like changing it up like that.'

The film became a huge critical and box office success, winning two Golden Globes and receiving four Oscar nominations – including Best Film.

Annette Bening said: 'This was something that we did have a hard time getting financing. Now it's nominated as best picture. It's part of what people are talking about. It's become part of our contemporary pop culture world.'

The *Guardian* wrote: 'Lisa Cholodenko's sparkling picture is an easygoing comedy of emotional difficulty, a witty portrait of postmodern family life in which script, casting, direction and location all just float together without any apparent effort at all.

'*The Kids Are All Right* shrewdly foregrounds and isolates the choices made in creating a family: choices which are usually unexamined. Couples generally get together, get pregnant, maybe stay together, or not: things happen too gradually to be noticeable. But the story of this ready-made bio-step-family is constructed in such a way that things happen suddenly and the choices are thrown into vivid, pin-sharp relief. Ruffalo's Paul himself starts to appear less sympathetic and less comic, and his interest in the family more parasitic, more that of an insidiously groovy emotional vampire. But at the same time, he shows himself poignantly, even tragically unprepared for the burdens of fatherhood thrust upon him. He can never go back to what he was before, and yet being absorbed into this family isn't easy. It is the hardest possible juggling act for director and performers alike: and yet Cholodenko and her cast carry it off with sensitivity, wit and warmth.'

U is for...

Universally Loved

Given the pedigree of the director and cast – a heady blend of veteran stars and up and comers – and the quality of the source material, it won't come as a surprise that *The Hunger Games* film wowed fans of the book. What Lionsgate were hoping for though is that it also appealed to non readers.

The Twilight Saga has made over $3 billion in global box office and DVD sales, and there is still another film to be released. *Harry Potter*'s success has easily doubled that. So you can see why *The Hunger Games'* success was so vital to Lionsgate. Their stock value has dropped alarmingly over the last few years, and market analyst James Marsh had this to say: '*The Hunger Games* could be the biggest catalyst for Lionsgate's profits and share price during the next decade. It could be a game changer for them.'

Costing $80 million to make, Lionsgate wisely decided to tone down the violence to ensure it got a lesser rating – meaning potentially more people could see it. 'We weren't going to let the violence be gratuitous or the selling point of the franchise,' said an executive from Lionsgate. 'This is an emotional story about a young girl who sacrifices everything and sets off a revolution she never intended.'

Luckily, appeal to the mainstream it did.

Talking about sequels, Lionsgate head Jon Feltheimer said before the film came out: '*The Hunger Games* must hit $100 million in domestic box office sales to justify making sequels. I'm not too concerned we won't get to that kind of number. There's just too much heat for this property around the world.'

His view was correct, and a sequel is in the works. In fact, work on the sequel was underway long before the film even came out! On 16 November 2011, *Deadline* reported: 'Lionsgate is getting serious about the second instalment of *The Hunger Games*. The mini-major is courting Oscar-winning *Slumdog Millionaire* scribe Simon Beaufoy to write *Catching Fire*, the second instalment of the three book series that tracks the life and death adventures of Katniss Everdeen (Jennifer Lawrence). Aside from *Slumdog Millionaire*, Beaufoy also scripted *127 Hours*, *The Full Monty* and most recently adapted *Salmon Fishing in the Yemen*.'

Gary Ross said: 'I love the title *Catching Fire*, because from the moment Katniss was willing to eat the berries, the moment she was willing to give her life for something larger than herself, she set off a chain reaction that was at once bigger than her and also because of her. That's a very exciting movie to make because you're seeing the emergence of a leader. It's the birth of a revolution so it has context that's larger than just the Games themselves.'

Lawrence says about the sequel: 'Signing onto the movies I was like: 'Well, I'll probably love the first one and then I'll just want to get the rest of them out of the way," she added. 'But I can't wait to start training. As soon as they said we'd need to start training in July, I was like "Woohoo!" I can't wait to get back. Though I don't know if that's because I think we might shoot in Hawaii…'

V is for...

Vanessa Hudgens

Josh Hutcherson had a short romance with his *Journey 2: The Mysterious Island* co-star Vanessa Hudgens. He told *Seventeen* magazine. 'Oh, boy. I don't know if "dating" is the right word. She's awesome. We love being together. When I first met her, we just really hit it off. We could be goofy and silly and not worry about anything except having fun. I adore her.'

They never officially confirmed their relationship and subsequently separated, with Hudgens telling the press: 'I think it's really important to love yourself and truly just be happy with yourself and just kind of let the rest of it fall into place. It is fun to go look at cute boys. But at the same time, I like being single. I feel like I have all this time for myself to be able to do these roles.' She is now reportedly dating actor Austin Butler.

However, the pair were shocked and left red faced during an Australian TV interview while promoting the film in early 2012. The interviewer hadn't realised they had split up, asking the visibly embarrassed pair: 'How long have you two been going out?' After a moment of excruciating silence, Hutcherson explained: 'We're not... We were at one point, but she broke my heart – no, just kidding. That was a while ago. We're just really good friends now.'

In another interview, when asked about whether he had a type, Hutcherson revealed: 'I like girls I can have deep conversations with. The meaning of life and existence – you can go on forever about that stuff. When girls play the ditzy-dumb thing I'm like: "Oh, God, please stop." For me it's all about being true to yourself and being real. I think if a girl tries to be something she's not to try to make you think otherwise of her, then that's just unattractive. I'd much rather be with somebody that's naturally who they are.'

Hutcherson said he also had instant chemistry with

Lawrence, but he conceded that playing a guy who is a big romantic wasn't hard, saying: 'I feel like every relationship I get into ends up being like that! I'm someone who can fall in love at the drop of a hat. My parents raised me to be very accepting of other people, so because of that, I feel like I might be overly accepting of girls. If a girls shows any interest, I'm like "Yes! I love you, you're amazing!"'

Despite his new-found hunk status, Josh Hutcherson is still looking for love – telling *Seventeen*: 'I don't think I've had love at first sight yet. But, I've definitely had moments where I've seen a person, and I'm like: "Wow, there is something different about you, and I really want to get to know you." I haven't really gained the courage to talk to those girls. I still get a little nervous when talking to girls. Which is awful, and embarrassing, because I feel like I shouldn't.'

Talking about his ideal date, he said: 'I'm a big fan of the beach. I think going to the beach is a great first date. It really can show you if the person is fun or not. Going to movies is fun but you don't get to talk to the person and get to know them. I'm into fun people and that's a good place to have fun with somebody.'

Vampires

Thanks to *Twilight*, vampires are big things in Hollywood. Josh Hutcherson starred in a movie hoping to capitalise on that success. The 2009 movie *Cirque du Freak: The Vampire's Assistant* is based on the book by Darren Shan. Hutcherson plays Steve, best friend to the film's main character Darren (played by Chris Massoglia), and their adventure starts when they go to a travelling freak show. Discovering a vampire at the show, played by John C. Reilly, Steve begs to become a member of the undead. Their actions eventually transpire to cause a rift between warring vampire clans, with Hutcherson ending up becoming one of the film's villains. He told *Teen Hollywood*: 'It was cool to play a bad guy. When I read the script, I read it early on before it got settled as to who was going to play what role. Darren was the lead role and that was interesting and I like the character a lot but, for me, I was more interested to play Steve because it was something I'd never really taken on before so it was great. I loved getting to play the bad guy and kind of unleash the evilness.'

Paul Weitz, who co-directed *American Pie*, uses the same tactic for this, casting relativity young performers who are not yet household names. He said: 'It's always fun for me to take kids who haven't really been seen widely before, and give them a huge part and lay all my chips on. From the first day, Chris and Josh seem to be building a natural friendship with each other, and that's a big part of our story: two kids who are really close friends who are going in totally different directions.'

Asked about the vampire trend, Hutcherson said: 'I think they're really cool and really hot. I'm a big fan of the older vampire movies like *The Lost Boys* and *Interview with the Vampire*, but I also like *Twilight* a lot. It's cool to play a vampire and be a part of this new, hot genre. Vampires can do what they want whenever they want, like fly around all the time. Plus, girls love vampires. Maybe they don't want to admit it, but they do, which is a plus.'

Reilly said about the film: 'One of the main appeals to the books is that Darren Shan doesn't treat kids like kids. He lets his readers experience a ton of stuff. The studio will market a movie based on what people think they know me as. The last couple of movies have been comedies, so I think they added a bit more comedy to the trailers than what's in the movie. There are comedic accents, but this movie is pretty serious and a bit scary.

'What Darren did in those books was the guide for everything. It's not like we made any decisions, character decisions, that were different from the books. In his world, the vampires are just people who can no longer be out in the daylight, they're super strong, they're able to drink blood to survive, but they don't have fangs. What I liked is that they're just people who lived a really long time, they're not like these supernatural characters. We puncture the [archetypal bubble] in the movie. I thought it'd be interesting to play someone who's born in the early 1800s and is still around now. Imagine what that would do to your brain. You've been through all of the changes in technology and all of that – what would that do? Are you wise? Cynical? Toying around with that. These vampires age slowly, but they're not immortal.'

The film wasn't a hit at the box office, and was met with a middling response by critics. But it was a chance for Hutcherson to make a horror movie, a genre he is a fan of. 'I love 'em! The *Saw* type of modern-day horror movie,' he told *Teen Hollywood*. 'I love getting scared and it takes a really good scary movie to scare me. One of my favourite modern-day vampire movies is *30 Days of Night*. That was so good. I loved those vampires. They were so different.'

Vietnam

One of the overriding experiences from *The Hunger Games* is its violence. 'Reading the books, I thought I understood the brutality,' said Hutcherson. 'But then you walk onto set and you see all the weapons in the Cornucopia and this little kid who's 10 years old. The movie can push Suzanne's idea to the furthest extent of just how messed up this totalitarian world is.'

Violence and war was something that has stuck closely with Collins. Her father had served in the Vietnam War and she knew deeply about the devastating effects of combat. She knew her father was in the war, and after watching cartoons as a kid sometimes news footage of the war would begin after her shows had ended and she would be distraught looking at the violent footage, knowing that her father was there.

She said: 'If your parent is deployed and you are that young, you spend the whole time wondering where they are and waiting for them to come home. As time passes and the absence is longer and longer, you become more and more concerned – but you don't really have the words to express your concern. There's only the continued absence.'

She explained about her dad. 'He was in the Air Force, a military specialist, a historian, and doctor of political science. When I was a kid, he was gone for a year in Vietnam. It was very important to him that we understood about certain aspects of life. So, it wasn't enough to visit a battlefield, we needed to know why the battle occurred, how it played out, and the consequences. Fortunately, he had a gift for presenting history as a fascinating story. He also seemed to have a good sense of exactly how much a child could handle, which is quite a bit.'

Mockingjay also deals with a character's struggle to cope with the memories of violence during battle, and she based that on her experiences with her dad's struggles coming back from the Vietnam War. She said she sometimes heard him in the middle of the night crying in his sleep after another nightmare.

The Vietnam War focused on a battle between North Vietnam and South Vietnam – with the former being supported by some communist countries and the latter counting the United States as one of its allies. Fearing a complete communist takeover of South Vietnam, the US army began serious involvement during the 1960s, peaking in 1968. After that, US forces began to withdraw. Nearly 60,000 service members were killed in the violent conflict.

Because of her childhood memories Collins is keen to show her readers that war isn't fun, and thinks it's important that they are educated. 'If we wait too long, what kind of expectation can we have? We think we're sheltering them,' she said. 'But what we're doing is putting them at a disadvantage. I don't write about adolescence. I write about war, for adolescents.

'My father felt that it was part of his responsibility to teach us, his children, about history and war. When I think back, at the centre of all this is the question of what makes a necessary war – at what point is it justifiable or unavoidable?

'One of my earliest memories is being at West Point military academy and watching the cadets drill on the field. If you went to a battleground with my father, you would hear what led up to the battle. You would hear about the war. You would have the battle re-enacted for you, I mean, verbally, and then the fallout from the battle.

'And having been in a war himself and having come from a family in which he had a brother in World War II and a father in World War I, these were not just distant or academic questions, they were very personal questions for him. He would discuss these things at a level that he thought we could understand and were acceptable for our age. But, really, he thought a lot was acceptable for our age, and I approach my books in the same way.'

W is for...

Woody Harrelson

Woody Harrelson is one of Hollywood's great survivors. Each decade has seen a new facet appear in his screen persona. Thanks to his breakthrough role as the ditzy bartender in the smash hit sitcom *Cheers*, Harrelson was one of TV's much loved stars. Desperate to free himself from that image, the nineties saw a different Woody Harrelson. Thanks to roles like the basketball hustler Billy Hoyle in *White Men Can't Jump* and as a serial killer in Oliver Stone's *Natural Born Killers*, Harrelson was the reluctant movie star.

The beginning of the millennium marked Harrelson

as a character actor, appearing in many films in a supporting role. If his screen time wasn't as long as the actors, it didn't seem to matter much, as he regularly enhanced or even stole any scene that he was in. Other notable roles include *No Country For Old Men*, *The People Vs Larry Flynt* and *The Walker* – the latter of which saw him play a gay man who escorts rich old ladies to events.

Born in Texas, Harrelson's early life is every bit as dramatic as some of his movies. His father was a contract killer and was convicted of killing a federal judge. He was sentenced to life prison, and eventually died there. Growing up the self confessed 'mama's boy' who was 'deeply mesmerised by the church', Harrelson eventually ended his dream job of studying the bible after he performed a u-turn, accusing the Bible of being just a document to control people. Instead, he set out to be an actor.

He joined the cast of *Cheers* in 1985, replacing Nicholas Colasanto, who played the much-loved Coach for three seasons before sadly dying in real life. Harrelson would play Woody for eight years, winning an Emmy.

Lately, Harrelson has been on a bit of a winning streak. His role as the cynical Tallahassee in *Zombieland* saw him score one of his biggest box office hits, while darker roles in *The Messenger* and the recent *Rampart* has led to critical acclaim and some acting gongs.

Cementing his success, he landed the role of Haymitch Abernathy in *The Hunger Games* movie. Typical of the actor's dedication to his craft, he made sure he read all the books. He loved reading them so much he insisted he couldn't put them down and has now made his entire family read them! Harrelson has never appeared in a sequel before, and he's now signed on for four movies.

He told MTV: 'I was interested because I knew Gary Ross was doing it. I love Gary; I think he's a great director and such an amazing guy. I didn't know about the books until after they offered me the part, and I took a while to respond. But then I started reading the first book and I really liked it. But, I thought about it and I just didn't think there was enough to do, it wasn't a huge part or anything. I'm happy to do smaller parts – I don't have a problem with that – but it just didn't seem like there was enough to do. I turned it down, but then Gary called me and said: "Dude, you've got to do this. I don't have a second choice. You've got to play Haymitch." And I was like: "Well, when you put it that way… let's do this damn thing!" And I'm so glad that I did, because it really was one of the best experiences and just a great group.'

Haymitch is a popular character in the series, and Harrelson was desperate that his performance had the same impact. He told the *LA Times*: 'It was my objective to give the character as much comedy as I could without it seeming not to fit, I tried to take a certain comedic aspect and give a sense, through that, that he's been through a lot and is anaesthetizing himself as a result of that.

'I didn't want it to feel like just because he's an alcoholic that he would look just like any bum on the street. So there are things that go against your expectation of what a washed-up guy would look like.'

Getting Haymitch's distinctive look came easy for the actor – he based it on his brother's hair. And by the end of the filming the first film, he seemed excited about being part of it. He may have had years of screen experience, but working on *The Hunger Games* seemed like a fulfilling experience for him. He told *Empire*: 'The sets are incredible, just amazing! Sometimes you don't notice the hair and make-up as much in a movie because it kind of blends in, but particularly in the Capitol there were some wild concepts. Pretty much every aspect of this production had the best people in the business, and it was just a pleasure to see what they came up with.'

Winter's Bone

Jennifer Lawrence plays Katniss in *The Hunger Games*, daughter to an absent father and an equally absent mother, forced to look after her younger sibling as they face starvation in the poverty stricken land. If you replace sibling with siblings you also have her career-making performance in *Winter's Bone*.

Directed by Debra Granik, it tells the story of a teenage girl named Ree who goes in the search for her drug dealer father after she learns he's jumped bail – an action that could cost them the house that he put up as collateral. John Hawkes plays Ree's uncle and he gives a sensational performance, matched easily by Lawrence. She is compelling as a young woman forced to make harrowing decisions for the good of her family. It is a performance this is packed full of both toughness and vulnerability.

Granik herself had been hailed as one to watch thanks to her blistering film debut *Down to the Bone*, which starred Vera Farmiga. As soon as she read Daniel Woodrell's book she knew it was perfect material for a film.

Talking to *Cinema Review*, the film's director said: 'I read *Winter's Bone* in one sitting. I had not done that with any book in a long time. I wanted to see how this girl, Ree, was going to survive. It felt like an old fashioned type of tale, with a character I couldn't help but root for, and with an atmosphere my mind was actively trying to conjure. It also felt fresh in that I do not often get a chance to imagine life like Ree's, whose circumstances lie outside the confines of my own.

'To launch this project, Anne Rosellini, the producer, and I met with Daniel Woodrell in his home base in Southern Missouri and embarked on our first scout with him. We looked at creeks, caves, and homes of all kinds. We photographed yards, roads, and woods. Katie Woodrell, Daniel's wife, arranged for us to meet singers, storytellers, folklorists, and all manner of scholars and practitioners steeped in Ozark culture – past and present. Also, we had an informative and heartbreaking discussion with the sheriff about what the meth problem has been like over the last two decades. After this visit, we were very enthused. We had also learned that to move forward we would need a guide, a local person who could carefully and respectfully introduce us to a community that might, over time, be persuaded to work with us.'

Granik looked at several young actresses, but none looked right for the material. They all looked too pretty and made up, and definitely didn't look like they had spent a long time in hard labour, fending on scraps.

She needed to look attractive, but believable as a girl that has spent time raising a family almost on her own.

Lawrence said: 'I loved it right away. I thought it was the best female role I ever read. I was fascinated with Ree and the story. And once I saw *Down to the Bone* I realised exactly how Debra wanted to shoot it, how real it was going to be and how kind of unrelenting. I knew it would be incredible.'

Granik said about Lawrence: 'Jen took this role into her heart and worked very hard to enter Ree's world. She used what she's got from her Kentucky roots – family that could help her with hunting, wood chopping, and other skills she wanted to have for the shoot. And to my ear, she already had a beautiful way of pronouncing American English that seemed right for Ree. Though the script had some very foreign phrases for us, Jen was familiar with some of them, having heard similar phrasing growing up. When she arrived in Missouri before the shoot, she worked closely with the life models and the family on whose property we shot the film. She learned how to operate the equipment, learned all the dog's names, and bonded with their children. In her role, she plays an older sister to a boy and a girl. Jen developed her own way of working with the kids. She made things real for them. She could also improvise and rehearse with them to put them at ease. Jen is very invested in working with her fellow actors and crew, which means she is always learning, absorbing, and challenging herself. I feel very lucky that we had the chance to make this film together.'

The reviews were universally positive, with Hawkes and Lawrence receiving the lion's share of praise.

Winter's Bone changed her life. On one occasion Steven Spielberg once stopped her in a corridor at DreamWorks to check that she was *the* Jennifer Lawrence – so impressed he was about her role in the movie.

Granik wasn't surprised, hailing: 'I think she will have a lot of offers to be in a huge amount of films. I think that people will respond to the fact, first of all, that she's had a very unusual early pathway, which is that she has not just been asked to play an attractive blonde. She has literally – in all the films she's been in – been asked to use her mind as well and to show a fully fledged character.

'So, if that can continue, that will be a very unusual trajectory. That will be much more like what happened to Jodie Foster, in the sense that Foster was enjoyed as someone who people could also rely on being a very intelligent person as well as, sometimes when she was young, endearing or cute or whatever.'

When asked about being hailed as the next big thing, Lawrence said: 'I don't know if there's any way you can be ready for it. Fame hits people differently when it happens suddenly. *Winter's Bone* could come out and I could have a nervous breakdown for all I know. But when people say that, I'm happy, it's a compliment. I never have given value to myself or viewed myself differently through my work, through my job. It doesn't give me a big head or anything. It just means I worked hard and it paid off. I'm grateful that people love the movie. But there were hundreds of people that went into making it, I'm just a tiny part.'

X is for...

X-Men: First Class

Following the success of *Winter's Bone*, Jennifer Lawrence was looking for a different project.

She said: 'I wanted to avoid being cast as the girl from *Winter's Bone*, to come out with something to counteract the total non-sexual, woollen-cap-pulled-over-my-eyes look of the movie and open myself up to do more things. You know, you've been watching a lot of dark, heavy movies and then all of a sudden you're like: "Ugh, I just need some crap!" I just wanted to do something that's fun. Not that that movie is stupid, but I would like to move on to do something different. Have a bigger trailer. Maybe wear make-up in a movie. I mean, that'd be crazy right? Me wearing make-up in a movie. Imagine that!'

That film would be *X-Men: First Class*. Directed by Matthew Vaughn, *X-Men: First Class* was a prequel based on the three hugely successful superhero movies. Set in the 1960s during the Cuban Missile Crisis, it focuses on the early relationship of Professor Charles Xavier and Magneto, played by Michael Fassbender and James McAvoy.

The first three films were huge successes for 20th Century Fox, and they made a successful spin-off movie featuring Wolverine – who is played by Hugh Jackman, and also features in *X-Men: First Class* as a cameo.

It was marked as a fresh beginning for the franchise, and it was a big success – earning $353 million. Talking about the film, director Matthew Vaughn said: 'In every film I do, I ask where the human angle is. Every character and action beat must have one. If I can slip in something that helps audiences connect with and care about the characters, it will only enhance the experience of watching the movie. If you don't care about the characters, then what's the point?

'*X-Men: First Class* has big ideas and big moments. We're not always relying on huge visual effects to make the movie work. The effects support the characters.

The film is a great character piece, with some huge action scenes.'

Producer Bryan Singer began thinking about an origins story when was directing the first two *X-Men* pictures. 'I would always think about the histories of the characters when telling the actors how to inform their behaviour. So to be able to go back and execute those back stories I had in my imagination was very satisfying. The magic of genre films is you can tell stories about the human condition from an unexpected vantage point, dressed up in spectacle and wonder. That's especially important for the *X-Men* films because that universe presents characters with a lot of depth. The best *X-Men* stories celebrate that complexity, and that's what we all wanted for this film.'

Recalling a chat with Patrick Stewart, the original actor who played Charles Xavier, Singer added: 'Patrick was wondering about the origins of Charles, and even then I had an idea about it, which was very different from the version in the comics, which was set in Tibet and involved an alien agent named Lucifer. And then I explained my ideas. Patrick said: "I prefer it your way!"'

Producer Lauren Shuler Donner, said: 'During the making of *X2* we were chatting between scenes about some of our younger cast members, and I said:

"Wouldn't it be great to see a young Professor X or Magneto. We should do a film about the X-Men when they were young." Everyone went: "Yeah, good idea, good idea." And so we all talked about it for quite a while, and then of course went back to making *X2*.'

Just like *The Hunger Games*, Lawrence was close to turning the franchise down because she wasn't sure about starring in a blockbuster movie. Lawrence mused: 'The *X-Men* movies are huge and then there are sequels, and it's hard to talk about doing a movie when there are sequels and you haven't read the script – what if I hate the script and have to make it three times? So I think the idea of sequels was the biggest concern for me, because I was thinking: "I have no idea where I'm going to be in my life when these movies come out. Am I going to regret this decision I impulsively made when I was 20?"

'Eventually I read the script – which they were guarding like it was the Holy Grail – and I think I was preparing for it to be bad. But it was actually really good, and I loved it. And it was going to star two of my favourite actors, Michael Fassbender and James McAvoy. Suddenly it became an easy decision.'

An easy decision bolstered by the complexity of her eventual character, the young shape shifter Raven. 'I thought the Raven Darkholme of the script was interesting, in that she was a normal young girl who was insecure and just discovering her sexuality, her womanhood and her power, and finally forms an opinion of her own at the end. I kind of liked watching her evolution.'

To give a quick background to *X-Men*: a mutant gene has been discovered, bestowing some humans with special gifts. However, humankind is understandably wary of such a discovery and views 'mutants' with a worried gaze. Professor Charles Xavier and Magneto are both mutants, but both share a differing view – the former wants mutants and humans to integrate with each other, while the latter believes mutants are part of the natural evolution and are the dominant species.

Raven is a shape shifter, with her natural form being an all blue creature. She is friends with and is besotted by Charles Xavier, her foster brother. Given the public's mistrust of mutants, she finds herself torn between her love for Xavier and Magneto's philosophy. Magneto tells her to embrace her mutant form and to stop hiding it to blend in.

Describing her character she told *IGN*: 'Raven, or Mystique, is a shape shifter, and when she is in her natural, blue, scaly, red-haired form she also has superhuman agility. She's young, and she's a normal teenager dealing with insecurities, but her insecurities aren't that normal. She's insecure about being a mutant, but she slowly grows to accept it and evolves into herself and starts to love it.'

She had not seen any of the previous movies, conceding: 'I was completely and totally caught off guard by it. Which is really stupid because it's one of the biggest franchises in the world, so I felt like an idiot, but as soon as I signed on the dotted line, it was very exciting. I watched the movies before my screen test, and for the comics I'm still getting through these two huge binders. It's going to take me years to get through just Mystique's parts. It's one of those things where you don't even know where to start. But I ask a lot of questions and I have taken a crash course which has helped.'

Former model Rebecca Romijn originally and memorably played the character in the original films, and Lawrence was reluctant to star in the film, conceding that the older actress was one of the most beautiful people in the world. After finally agreeing to the part, she went on a diet and two hour daily work out to get the right physique. The laborious make-up also took eight hours. 'I just got tired thinking about it. It was a long process.'

As stated before, Lawrence wanted the part after seeking something lighter after several dramatic roles. And she certainly got that, saying: 'It was mostly just fun. I don't remember us working, I just remember us cracking up on set.'

Joining her were January Jones, who was shocked after reading the script, realising that it was set in the same period as the sixties-era TV hit *Mad Men*. 'I thought oh, god, you must be kidding me!' she recalled, laughing. 'I was really excited about being part of the incredible world of X-Men. It was something very new for me to combine all the physical challenges the role offered, as well as the dramatic aspects. My character Emma is technically a villain, but I think her motives are genuine and from the heart. She thinks she is doing what is best for her race and will do whatever it takes to keep mutants alive and form a stronger species.'

The other villain is Sebastian Shaw, played by Kevin Bacon. 'Shaw is an extremely powerful man and essentially a sociopath. But he sincerely believes that he is trying to create a better world, without humans, run and populated entirely by mutants. Conventional morality does not apply to Shaw. In his mind he believes that mutants and humans will never be able to live together, so it is survival of the fittest, and Shaw is determined to protect the mutant race. He is driven by his firm belief that he thinks he is the right leader for the new world.'

The film received huge praise from critics, with *Total Film* praising Lawrence's vulnerability, and *Cinema Blend* stating: '*X-Men: First Class* feels spry and self-contained, a blast of colourful and passionate enthusiasm with just enough weight to matter. It feels phenomenal to have these mutants back.' *Hollywood Reporter* added: 'As the naturally blue-skinned, red-haired and yellow-eyed Raven/Mystique, Lawrence is at her most appealing when conveying an ashamed insecurity about her natural looks, which she can conceal with a human façade.'

Empire magazine however, wasn't that enthused, bemoaning: 'It is so single-mindedly plot-driven that it whips along at too brisk a pace, rushing through scenes to an end point which feels too neat, too wrapped up, too contrived for a story which still has at least 40 years to go before we get to *X-Men*.'

A sequel is on the cards, with Simon Kinberg on writing duties. Producer Bryan Singer said about his hopes for the sequel: 'I don't know if every movie has to be a history lesson. But there's a lot of history to cover. If we sequelised this, it could inhabit a whole world of the 20th century. When *First Class* happened,

Kennedy had not been assassinated and the Vietnam War hadn't even happened yet.

What's really interesting about the 1960s setting is the civil rights movement. What's fascinating about these two characters is that they're really the Malcolm X and Martin Luther King of comic mythology.'

Y is for...

Young Adult Novels

In recent years young adult books have become increasingly successful, following something of a slump in the nineties, with critics deriding them as becoming formulaic and plodding. This is a genre that is growing and growing, and has seen books written for teenagers but are as equally popular with adults as well. Reasons for that are attributed to more sophisticated writing and original ideas – like the *Twilight*, *Gossip Girl* and *The Hunger Games* novels. The current young adult novels also have racier content than before.

It's common opinion that it was the sixties and

seventies that saw the beginnings of young adult novels, thanks to the popular book series by Judy Blume. But there is an even bigger boom at hand at the moment, according to *Booklist* magazine critic, Michael Cart: 'Kids are buying books in quantities we've never seen before, and publishers are courting young adults in ways we haven't seen since the 1940s. We are right smack-bang in the new golden age of young adult literature.'

An article by *GreatSchools.org* stated: 'Young adult books typically feature a tween or teen protagonist and deals with topics favoured by this age range: fantasy, adventure and coming-of-age stories. Recently, more graphic sex and violence has crept into books aimed at the younger YA age ranges, causing concern and consternation among parents.'

'Authors realise that teens are exploring the edges of experience, and young adult books explore reality to the extreme,' said a representative for the Teen Services Coordinator for the San Francisco Public Library. 'Within the explosion of young adult literature there have been some books that explore sexuality more graphically than in the past. In the past five years, more books are pushing the limit to explore themes of at-risk teens and teens on the edge.'

One parent who has criticised this trend, however, is

author Barbara Feinberg, who wrote about young adult books. She said: 'The books that were being assigned were very topical and dark, with topics such as maternal suicide, alcoholism, family dysfunction and abandonment. I would never want to censor things – I think kids should read what they want – but it seemed there was a preponderance of these kinds of things in young adult literature, and it was all kind of contrived.'

Z is for...

Zathura

According to the film's production notes:

> After their father (Tim Robbins) leaves for work, leaving them in the care of their older sister (Kristen Stewart), six year-old Danny (Jonah Bobo) and ten-year old Walter (Josh Hutcherson) either get on each other's nerves or are totally bored.
>
> When their bickering escalates and Walter starts chasing him, Danny hides in a dumbwaiter. But Walter surprises him, and in retaliation, lowers Danny into their dark, scary basement, where he

discovers an old tattered metal board game, called *Zathura*. After trying unsuccessfully to get his brother to play the game with him, Danny starts to play on his own.

From his first move, Danny realises this is no ordinary board game. His spaceship marker moves by itself and when it lands on a space, a card is ejected, which reads: "Meteor shower, take evasive action." The house is immediately pummelled from above by hot, molten meteors.

When Danny and Walter look up through the gaping hole in their roof, they discover, to their horror, that they have been propelled into deepest, darkest outer space. And they are not alone…

So begins an exhilarating, sometimes frightening, but always unpredictable adventure. Danny and Walter realise that unless they finish the game they'll be trapped in outer space forever. With every turn, they confront one incredible obstacle after another: They accidentally put their sister Lisa into a deep cryonic sleep, are chased by a crazed, malfunctioning six-foot robot, rescue a stranded astronaut (Dax Shepard) and are besieged by lizard-like, carnivorous creatures called Zorgons.

With the help of the astronaut, Danny and

Walter begin to put their petty fraternal differences aside, work together to overcome the obstacles they encounter and attempt to finish the game so they can go home.

But all their efforts may be in vain when they face their biggest challenge of all – a battle against an intense gravitational pull into the void of the dark planet Zathura.

Director Jon Favreau said: 'When I first read the script, I was immediately taken by how sincere the depiction of the characters was. David (Koepp) and John (Kamps) preserved a great deal of the emotion and imagery of Chris's book.

'I wanted *Zathura* to work first and foremost on a visceral level, very much in the way Steven Spielberg's early Amblin movies did. Films like *E.T.* and *Close Encounters* and George Lucas's *Star Wars* movies are the kind of sci-fi stories I grew up loving, and that's something I was eager to explore with this film. I also thought it would be fun to work with special effects, miniatures, robots, computer graphics – areas I haven't had a chance to play with in the past. After working on *Elf* and having a small taste of that kind of filmmaking, *Zathura* seemed to be the next logical step for me to challenge myself and grow as a filmmaker.

'I have two children now, I watch a lot of movies that are geared towards kids and this one really appealed to my sensibilities. As a filmmaker, a big part of your job is to put energy into getting a message out into the world that you believe in. I like stories that offer hope and films that have responsible themes. When you're making a movie for young people, there should be a little aspirin in the apple sauce. There should be a nice message at the core.'

Esteemed film critic Roger Ebert noted: 'What makes this fun is that Danny and Walter are obviously not going to get hurt. Alien fire blasts away whole chunks of their house, but never the chunks they're in, and the giant lizards seem more preoccupied with overacting than with eating little boys. The young actors, Hutcherson and Bobo, bring an unaffected enthusiasm to their roles, fighting with each other like brothers even when threatened with roasting by a solar furnace. Their father, I should have mentioned, is played by Tim Robbins, although his role consists primarily of being absent. Kristen Stewart makes the most of the sister, Lisa's, non-cryonic scenes. And then there is the character of the Astronaut (Dax Shepard), who materialises at a crucial point and helps shield the kids from intergalactic hazards. Lisa's crush on the Astronaut becomes cringy after all is known.

'*Zathura* lacks the undercurrents of archetypal menace and genuine emotion that informed *The Polar Express*, a true classic that is being re-released again this year. But it works gloriously as space opera. We're going through a period right now in which every video game is being turned into a movie, resulting in cheerless exercises such as *Doom*, which mindlessly consists of aliens popping up and getting creamed. *Zathura* is based on a different kind of game, in which the heroes are not simply shooting at targets, but are actually surrounded by real events that they need to figure out. They are active heroes, not passive marksmen. Nobody even gets killed in *Zathura*. Well, depending on what happens to the lizards on the other side of the black hole.'